To Dale –

Enjoy! Norey
2024

Inside Norey's Kitchen

Inside Norey's Kitchen

A Collection of Recipes from Newport, Rhode Island

by Norey Dotterer Cullen

Jostens

Copyright © 2023 by Norey Dotterer Cullen
All rights reserved. This book or any portion thereof may not be reproduced or used in any manner whatsoever without the express written permission of the publisher except for the use of brief quotations in a book review.

Printed by Jostens, Clarksville TN
https://printing.jostens.com/

Design by Shelley Kornatz Shaw
Photography by Matthew Cullen & Peter Walsh
Production by Peter Walsh

First Printing, 2023
ISBN 979-8-218-13937-7
Copies available: www.blackpearlnewport.com

Table of Contents

THANK YOU! 7

NOREY'S STORY 8

A NOTE FROM NOREY 10

THE CUPBOARD ESSENTIALS 13

HORS D'OEUVRES 15

SOUPS 41

SALADS 67

SANDWICHES 89

ENTRÉES 101

VEGETABLES 125

DRESSINGS & SAUCES 135

BREAD PUDDINGS 145

     SAVORY 146

     SWEET 151

CAKES 159

COOKIES 175

DESSERTS 189

APPENDIX 198

RECIPE INDEX 200

Thank You!

I want to express my heartfelt thanks to our many friends and family members who offered encouragement and advice in each stage of this book's development. It's been a journey that has brought so many together for dinners, summer barbecues, holiday gatherings, birthday celebrations, and more. Going forward, their support in spreading the word about this first cookbook will be forever remembered!

I also want to thank our gifted designer, Shelley Kornatz Shaw. She could not have been more creative and professional in every stage of this production. She has the patience of an angel!

My son, Matthew, has provided his support and help with photography. He captured the cover photo, plus the one below of Peter and me, and other select recipe shots throughout the book.

Finally, I couldn't have done this book without my devoted partner, Peter Walsh. He has been my rock, encouraging me every step of the way and helping me with organization, pictures, editing, and so much more. He is my constant hero!!

Norey's Story

Norey Dotterer Cullen, born and raised in Newport, Rhode Island, has been involved in the food industry for most of her adult life. After opening a fast-food restaurant in 1971, Norey and her husband, Tom, bought The Black Pearl Restaurant in 1974 (blackpearlnewport.com). It is located on the waterfront in Newport, Rhode Island, and became a landmark establishment for eating and spirits during the famous America's Cup Races.

In 1986 Norey and her sister, Nina, established *Dotterer's Ltd.* featuring their own gourmet food products including mustard, hot pepper jelly, caramel bourbon sauce, seafood sauce, and a sweet balsamic vinaigrette. These were sold throughout the East Coast to gourmet food stores such as Zabar's® in New York City.

Norey has been involved with food and cooking since she was a young child, learning from her mother, Evelyn Dotterer, who was a superb cook in her own right. With over 40 years of experience in the food industry, Norey's background provided the foundation for opening her own restaurant in Newport in 2000. "Norey's" became an immediate success! She bought a diner and refurbished the entire restaurant, creating a warm, cozy bistro featuring home-style menus with all fresh ingredients... Basically like eating at home!

Norey wanted people to be able to come in black tie or blue jeans, and enter into a very friendly environment — so much so that people would just start talking to other diners next to them because the atmosphere warranted it. She had her son Matthew build her a long table in the center of the restaurant, calling it the "strangers" table. Multiple people sat not knowing each other. It became "the place" to sit! Music was also a big part of the restaurant, playing classic songs from Frank Sinatra, Judy Garland, James Taylor, and lots of "oldies but goodies".

Food was the #1 component to the success of "Norey's"! Norey started with her well-known soups and salads; all simple but very tasty. Meatloaf, creamy mashed potatoes sprinkled with fresh snipped chives, roasted brussel sprouts, and roasted plum tomatoes with grated parmesan cheese and basil, was just one example of a fall night's dinner. Norey also became known for her wide range of delicious desserts. Her Baked Caramelized Pears and Chocolate Raisin Sticky Toffee Pudding Cake are just two examples of Norey's luscious "never too full to have one" desserts.

Norey turned her restaurant over to her son, Tyler, in 2015. She has been asked many times to come out with her own cookbook, and is now embarking on that task. This book includes recipes collected from Norey's grandmother, mother, sisters, and friends, but primarily come from her own experience as a chef, mother of four boys, and restauranteur.

A Note from Norey

It has been a real journey writing this cookbook. I've had a bittersweet time looking over my Mother's recipes, of which she had many. Just seeing her handwriting brought back so many memories of me and my two older sisters, Nancy and Nina, helping her in the kitchen. She had a large cake tin there, and every day I would come home and look under it… <u>always</u> finding something new to snack on. I don't know how she did it!!!

Growing up, we always opened and closed the "icebox" to grab salad items, milk, etc. The word "icebox" is special to me for all its memories, so I've decided to use it throughout this cookbook. For our younger readers who may not be familiar with an icebox, it actually is the refrigerator!

My Father was always bringing people home from his golf club in the early evening… Unannounced, of course! My Mother would go look in the icebox, pull out a few things, grab some ingredients from the pantry, and a delicious meal would appear in a short amount of time. That is why I have my own cupboard essentials which are so important, and listed on page 13 in this book. I feel she invented this idea long before it was popular!!

One of the most confusing things to me about cooking is not *HOW* to cook something, but rather deciding *WHAT* to cook. I have so many pages turned down in my cookbooks that I get frustrated as to what to make… Once I DECIDE what to make… then it is easy.

I love casual dining. We always have dinners in the kitchen or, weather permitting, outside. I turned my formal dining room into a downstairs bedroom when I had my knee replaced, and it has stayed that way. I have a decent-size kitchen and although it is casual dining, I do set a pretty table with flowers, and I love to decorate the table depending on the season or holiday. Actually, I set my table <u>first</u>, and love creating something unique and different for each meal. Then… I feel ready to start cooking!

I keep a notebook with information on my dinner parties and luncheons. It consists of who attended, what I served, what wine was paired with the food, and what the table settings were like. I write the date and the weather, too. It really helps as I can look back on my notes and not have any "repeats" on my menus. I always try to change the company and mix in a few acquaintences with my really good friends. I never worry if there are any extra guests, but in order for me to enjoy the party I have to be organized. A number of these recipes are for 8 servings. In most cases, one can cut ingredients in half if you are only serving 4–5 people.

A few last comments: (1) I don't measure much, so I have tried to give accurate measurements, but they might *not* be perfect. And (2), although I've grown up and live in Newport, I've never been a lover of seafood. This is crazy but it explains the limited recipes here!

Finally, I want to dedicate this cookbook to my four sons, Keith, Tyler, David, and Matthew, who are all "cooks" in their own right. I started this book as a collection to give to them so they would have a few family favorites, and it grew from there.

The Cupboard Essentials

You will find in many cookbooks that the author will write his or her rendition of ingredients which they feel are necessary to have on hand. If you're like me, I will start to cook something and invariably be out of at least one item. It gets me crazy! So before you start cooking, make sure you have all the ingredients you need.

Here is my list of "essentials":

> Eggs
> Butter
> Kosher Salt & Cracked Pepper
> Flour
> Oatmeal
> Cream
> Sour Cream
> Cream Cheese
> Hellmann's® Mayonnaise
> Granulated Sugar
> Confectioner's Sugar
> Brown Sugar
> Pure Vanilla Extract
> Chicken and/or Beef Broth
> Chocolate Chips (milk and dark)
> Fresh Garlic (fresh only!)
> Golden Raisins and Fresh Dates/Apricots
> Onions and Shallots
> Good Quality Olive Oil
> Vinegar (balsamic, white, and apple cider)
> Limes, Lemons, and Fresh Herbs
> Bottled Lemon Juice and Lime Juice
> Almonds and Pecans
> Ginger (fresh and crystallized)

HORS D'OEUVRES

Hors d'Oeuvres

Frankly, I could eat only hors d'oeuvres and skip dinner altogether. There are so many recipes out there. I'm always looking for new ideas and looking through cookbooks for something that catches my eye. I especially like to serve one-bite hors d'oeuvres... two bites at the most.

I realize that hors d'oeuvres are labor intensive, and many have to be made at the last minute... But they are well worth it! Different varieties of tea sandwiches are my favorite. I use thin sliced bread, such as Pepperidge Farm® white or wheat. It is ideal for these little gems. There are so many different fillings which I have listed in the following pages. They are perfect, especially in the summer.

What you choose to put into your sandwiches depends on the season and the occasion. <u>It is a *must* to cut the crusts off the sandwiches.</u> I assemble them on a pretty platter, usually placing them on a white doily. After I assemble the platter, I take several lengths worth of paper towel and wet it with water. Then I squeeze it out and gently unravel it. I place this on top of the sandwiches, making sure they're completely covered, then wrap the entire platter with saran wrap to ensure freshness. Before serving, I usually garnish the platter with a flower, fresh herbs, or a piece of fruit, then keep them in the icebox until ready to serve. For the best presentation, arrange your hors d'oeuvres on attractive platters, wooden boards, or a large Lazy Susan.

It's always good to have a few ready-made hors d'oeuvres on hand for pop-in guests — for example mixed nuts, to which you can add chocolate chips, raisins, or coconut to doctor them up. For popcorn, try adding truffle powder, powdered parmesan cheese, oregano, cumin... Just make sure you do *NOT* put nuts or salted popcorn into a silver dish. It will tarnish!

If you are serving a vegetable platter, make sure you put the cut vegetables in cold water in the icebox to get them really crisp before serving. Serve with a tiny bowl filled with your favorite dip, hummus, or kosher salt.

Basil & Tomato Rounds

SERVES: 10

(optional) 8 pieces of bacon (cooked crisp & chopped)

1 pint seasonal sweet cherry tomatoes (room temperature)

½ cup Hellmann's® mayonnaise

1 loaf soft bread of your choice

1 bunch fresh basil

snipped fresh chives

salt and pepper

small circle cookie cutter

Norey's Note:

I like using a small round cookie cutter to create circular sandwiches, but you could also make stars, flowers, or hearts... The possibilities are endless!

These are so simple, but are still one of my favorites.

TO PREPARE:

With a small round cookie cutter (about the size of a half-dollar), cut out circles from bread. Spread a generous portion of mayonnaise on each circle and add a folded piece of fresh basil.

Slice cherry tomatoes in half and drain on a paper towel. Put one half on each circle, on top of the basil. Stack a few pieces of cooked bacon on the tomatoes, then sprinkle the sandwiches with chives, salt, and pepper to finish. Assemble on a pretty plate with a doily liner.

P.S. I always keep my tomatoes out at room temperature. I cover them with a cloth to avoid getting fruit flies.

HORS D'OEUVRES

HORS D'OEUVRES

Cream Cheese Cinnamon Sticks

MAKES 3 DOZEN

1 stick unsalted butter

2 loaves Pepperidge Farm® thin bread

2 8-ounce blocks of cream cheese

2 tablespoons sugar

½ tablespoon cinnamon

Dipping Sauce:

8 ounces sour cream

2 teaspoons brown sugar

TO PREPARE:

Remove all crusts from bread, and roll crustless slices with a rolling pin so they are as thin as possible. (This is not hard, just a bit time-consuming.)

Spread a thin layer of softened cream cheese all over the bread. Roll the slice up like a pencil. Repeat this process until all the bread is prepared. Melt the butter and coat each roll with melted butter. Mix the cinnamon and sugar together on a plate, and coat each roll with the sweet mixture. Bake the sticks on a baking sheet at 350°F for 10 minutes.

Combine sour cream and brown sugar in a small bowl. Cut bread sticks in half and serve on a pretty platter with the dipping sauce on the side. These are delicious!

Norey's Note:

This recipe is from my friend Nancy Powell. I had this dish at one of her many special parties, and she kindly gave me the recipe.

These are a nice appetizer for a summer party or brunch!

Cream Cheese Dip with Almonds & Endive

SERVES: 6

1/2 cup golden raisins (or more)

2 8-ounce packages cream cheese (softened)

3 ounces bleu cheese (or more, good quality)

1 teaspoon horseradish

1 tablespoon chutney

1 tablespoon Worcestershire sauce

2 tablespoons chives (fresh, chopped)

1 cup sliced almonds (toasted)

3 endive

(optional) crackers or fresh vegetables

TO PREPARE:

Mix together all ingredients except endive until well-combined. Put the mixture into a glass bowl. Thinly slice the endive and serve alongside for dipping, or you can spread the dip on the endive and serve your guests the dressed leaves.

If you don't love endive, this dip also tastes great with carrots or hard crackers arranged on a platter!

HORS D'OEUVRES

Deviled Eggs

MAKES 2 DOZEN DEVILED EGGS

1 dozen eggs (I prefer small eggs)

1 tablespoon Hellmann's® mayonnaise

½ teaspoon dry mustard

½ teaspoon cider vinegar

salt and pepper

TO PREPARE:

Place eggs into a large pan of HOT water and boil for about 12–13 minutes. Take the eggs out and immediately put into a bowl of ice cold water.

Carefully remove shells from cooled eggs and slice in half lengthwise. Remove the hardened yolks from each halved egg and set aside in a bowl. Mix the rest of the ingredients together with the yolks. I put my egg yolks in a food processor and pulse a few times to make them fine.

Different toppings include adding curry (about 1 teaspoon), caviar, fresh dill, bacon, chopped tomatoes, smoked salmon, capers, sliced avocado, sliced sweet pickles, and scallions.

Fresh Dates with Cream Cheese & Almonds

SERVES: 6

12 fresh dates

24 salted almonds (or any large tree nut)

1 8-ounce package of cream cheese (softened)

TO PREPARE:

Slice dates in half and remove seed. Add a dab of softened cream cheese onto each half of the date, and top with an almond.

You can also top each halved date with a small piece of crispy bacon or a salted cashew.

Hummus (My Way!)

SERVES: 8

Norey's Note:

I am so glad that I love hummus, as it is so good for you and a great source of protein.

1 ½ cans Goya® chickpeas

2 tablespoons tahini

2 tablespoons olive oil

1 teaspoon garlic (minced)

2 tablespoons lemon juice

1 tablespoon lime juice

1 bunch cilantro (chopped)

½ pint yellow and red cherry tomatoes (seeded, chopped & drained of excess juice)

1 red pepper (chopped)

½ avocado (chopped)

3 scallions (thinly sliced)

1 teaspoon kosher salt and pepper

TO PREPARE:

Remove the thin skin on the chickpeas and rinse under cold water. Place chickpeas in a food processor along with tahini, olive oil, lemon juice, and lime juice, and process until smooth. Toast garlic in a small pan for 2 minutes or until slightly cooked, then add to mixture. If the hummus is too thick, just add a bit of water to thin it out.

Put the plain hummus on a small platter and then layer the cilantro, tomatoes, and scallions on top, making sure that the vegetables are evenly distributed. Finish with chopped avocado and chopped red pepper.

I like to top my finished hummus with a sprinkle of cumin and serve with good toasted pita chips.

HORS D'OEUVRES

Hungarian Cheese Spread

SERVES: 8

1 8-ounce package cream cheese (room temperature)

1 stick butter (room temperature)

8 ounces feta cheese

chopped chives

chopped parsley

1 English cucumber (thinly sliced)

1 loaf Pepperidge Farm® bread

Norey's Note:

I use this spread on so many sandwiches and as a base for hors d'oeuvres. So simple!!

TO PREPARE:

Put cream cheese, butter, and feta cheese into a food processor and blend thoroughly. Put mixture into a bowl and fold in the chives and parsley.

Take a small round cookie cutter and cut circles out of the bread, avoiding the crust. Spread a good amount of the cheese mixture onto each circle of bread. Top with a slice of cucumber and another small pinch of cheese mixture. Sprinkle some more chopped chives on top to garnish.

Kielbasa Bites with White Wine

SERVES: 6

1 pound kielbasa (sliced)

2 tablespoons brown sugar

1 tablespoons dijon mustard

1 cup white wine

3 tablespoons brandy

3 cloves garlic (chopped)

1 bunch Italian parsley (chopped)

1 tablespoon coarse black pepper

TO PREPARE:

Slice kielbasa on an angle and arrange in a large frying pan. Pour in white wine. Bring to a boil and cook until the wine is almost gone. Stir in brown sugar, mustard, and brandy. Cook for a few minutes, then turn off the heat and mix in the parsley and cracked pepper.

To serve, arrange finished kielbasa bitesin a small dish and set out toothpicks or crackers for guests to help themselves.

Norey's Note:

This is an easy recipe and men seem to love it.

HORS D'OEUVRES

Mini BLTs with Avocado

1 pint sweet cherry tomatoes (medium-sized)

½ cup Hellmann's® mayonnaise

1 bunch fresh basil (chopped)

1 pound bacon (cooked crisp, crumbled)

1 avocado

1 bunch scallions (finely chopped)

½ teaspoon kosher salt & pepper

Norey's Note:

Getting fresh, <u>seasonal</u> cherry tomatoes is a MUST! It makes a huge difference!

TO PREPARE:

Cut the tops off of the tomatoes and scoop out seeds with a small spoon. Turn them over and arrange on a paper towel to drain for several minutes. Slice a small sliver off the bottom end of the tomato just so it sits flat on a plate. Inside each tomato, layer a small dollop of mayonnaise, a pinch of fresh basil, and bacon crumbles. Top with a slice of avocado, and garnish the tomatoes with salt, pepper, and scallions.

These will fly off the plate so make a lot of these little darlings!

HORS D'OEUVRES

Mini Ham Salad Bites

MAKES 3 DOZEN MINI SANDWICHES

1 pound Boar's Head® honey ham

½ cup Hellmann's® mayonnaise

1 tablespoon sweet mustard

2 tablespoons sweet pickle relish

2 loaves Pepperidge Farm® bread (thin)

TO PREPARE:

Place ham in a food processor and pulse <u>a few times</u> to chop. Drain the pickle relish and pat dry with a paper towel. Stir relish, mayonnaise, and mustard into the chopped ham. Use a small round cookie cutter to cut out circles and put a spoonful of ham mixture on each circle to make a little open-faced sandwich. Top with a small slice of sweet pickle.

OR

Spread mixture on bread, then cut off crusts. Cut sandwich into quarters either cross-wise or diagonally. Stand them up on a tray with filling showing.

Norey's Note:

These little bites are always a hit if you like ham.

I like using a round cookie cutter to create circular sandwiches. You could also make stars, flowers, or hearts... The possibilities are endless!

Mini Roasted Potatoes

SERVES: 8

2 bags mini potatoes
1 stick butter
½ cup olive oil
1 tablespoon kosher salt
1 tablespoon pepper
(optional) 4 cloves garlic

Norey's Note:

I got so excited when I saw these tiny little potatoes at the store. Keep your eyes open for them in the produce section.

Really simple to make and they are gone in a minute!

TO PREPARE:

Melt butter in a small pan. Add garlic and olive oil, and cook for a few minutes until garlic is lightly toasted. Remove from heat and put into a large bowl. Add potatoes to bowl and toss thoroughly.

Line a half-sheet pan with aluminum and place coated potatoes on pan. Bake in oven at 400°F for 25 minutes or until soft. Shake the pan once or twice while they cook to get all sides crisp. Remove from oven and serve with your favorite dip. You can also garnish with finely chopped fresh cilantro, parsley, or basil.

HORS D'OEUVRES

Nana's German Meatballs

SERVES: 8

Norey's Note:

My mother made these little treats for so many occasions, but especially at Christmas.

Great as a meal over your favorite pasta, or as an appetizer with almost any sauce options!

1 pound ground beef

1 pound ground pork

1 pound ground veal

1 large onion (diced)

2 packages Knorr's® vegetable soup mix

3 cups bread crumbs (pref. homemade)

2 eggs (slightly beaten)

¼ cup half-and-half (optional)

3 tablespoons Worchestershire sauce

1 teaspoon basil & oregano (dried)

1 bunch fresh parsley (chopped)

2 teaspoons kosher salt & pepper

TO PREPARE:

Mix all ingredients together in a very large bowl. Roll a small amount in your hands to make a ball with the diameter of a quarter. Place the balls close together on a half-sheet pan lined with aluminum foil.

Bake meatballs at 350°F for 15-20 minutes or until golden brown and cooked through. Let cool. Place in a nice shallow bowl and serve with toothpicks. Meatballs can also be put into a freezer bag and frozen until ready to serve. To reheat, put on a sheet pan and warm at 300°F for 15 minutes. Serve with a toothpick.

Variation: Mix a pint of sour cream, 2 tablespoons Worcestershire sauce, and a bottle of Major Grey's® chutney together and toss with meatballs. Your favorite BBQ sauce or Italian marinara would work well, too!

Nina's Onion Cornbread

SERVES: 6

- 1 stick butter
- 1 cup onion (chopped)
- 1 egg (beaten)
- ½ cup milk
- 1 8-ounce can creamed corn
- 1 package corn muffin mix

- 1 ½ cup sour cream
- 1 cup sharp cheddar cheese
- (optional) 1 teaspoon tabasco
- salt & pepper
- (optional) 2 jalapeño peppers

TO PREPARE:

Melt butter and sauté chopped onions. Mince jalapeño peppers (if using) and combine with muffin mix, egg, milk, creamed corn, and tabasco. Mix in the butter and onions, and spread batter in a greased 8-inch square pan.

Shred the cheddar cheese. Spread sour cream, salt, and cheese carefully over batter.

Bake at 400°F for 30 minutes or until a toothpick in the center comes out clean. Cut into squares and serve.

Norey's Note:

If you want a "kick" to this cornbread, finely chop jalapeños and sauté for several minutes before adding to batter.

The peppers add great flavor!

HORS D'OEUVRES

Pear & Goat Cheese Bruschetta

3 ounces prosciutto

1 pear (skin on, sliced thin)

2 ounces fresh honey goat cheese

1 small loaf ciabatta bread

1 jar fig jam

blueberries (garnish)

2 ounces fresh parmesan (shaved)

TO PREPARE:

Cut ciabatta loaf into ½-inch slices and place on a baking sheet. Lightly toast in the oven at 375°F for 3 minutes. Spread a layer of goat cheese on each piece.

Wrap a slice of prosciutto around a slice of pear and place on top of goat cheese. Top with a small dollop of fig jam and garnish with shaved parmesan and blueberries. Delicious and pretty!

HORS D'OEUVRES

Roasted Plum Tomato Bruschetta

12 <u>small</u> plum tomatoes (halved)

3 tablespoons olive oil

1 bunch fresh basil (chopped)

8 ounces goat cheese (good quality, <u>softened</u>)

1 teaspoon oregano

1 teaspoon Kosher salt & pepper

1 loaf ciabatta bread (thinly sliced)

Norey's Note:

These are easy to make and delicious.

If you don't like goat cheese, try <u>fresh</u> mozzarella instead!

TO PREPARE:

Place halved tomatoes on a sheet pan lined with aluminum foil. Pour olive oil over tomatoes then sprinkle with oregano, salt, and pepper. Bake at 400°F for 20 minutes or until tomatoes have a "grilled" appearance. Set aside.

Arrange bread slices on a sheet pan and bake in the same oven for about 3 minutes. Watch closely so the bread doesn't burn. Let cool.

Spread goat cheese on bread and arrange a basil leaf and tomato halves on top. Garnish with a sprinkle of fresh basil, salt, and pepper.

Special Chicken Salad

SERVES: 4

4 pieces boneless chicken (cooked)

1 head Boston lettuce

(optional) 1 bunch red grapes (quartered)

½ cup celery (finely chopped)

1 teaspoon sweet mustard

½ cup Hellmann's® mayonnaise (or more)

1 loaf ciabatta or thin white bread

½ cup almonds (toasted)

½ cup dried apricots (chopped small)

1 tablespoon fresh tarragon

½ teaspoon kosher salt and pepper

TO PREPARE:

Cook the chicken and then chop into small pieces in a food processor. Mix all ingredients together except grapes and lettuce, reserving ½ tablespoon fresh tarragon for a garnish. Add mayonnaise to adjust the consistency to your liking.

For an hors d'oeuvre, use a medium round cookie cutter to cut out circles from bread. Top with mayonnaise, lettuce, and chicken salad. Garnish with a sprinkle of tarragon, apricot, or a halved grape.

OR

For tea sandwiches, put a <u>dab</u> of mayonnaise on one side of each slice of bread. Add lettuce to one side and chicken salad on the other. Remove crusts and cut into triangles.

Norey's Note:

You can also forego bread entirely in this recipe and serve the chicken salad on small pieces of lettuce or baby spinach. Garnish with microgreens on top!

HORS D'OEUVRES

SOUPS

Soups

There is nothing more provocative or delicious than a hot bowl of soup. Fresh ingredients are, to me, <u>essential</u> to turn a really good soup into a *great* soup! There is only one exception, and that is I use canned plum tomates when making tomato soup. I always start out with celery and onions, and I sauté them until soft and translucent. Depending on the soup, I sauté vegetables in olive oil or butter. I NEVER use MSG and rarely add flour to thicken soup. Instead, I thicken soup with cooked puréed potatoes or cooked puréed white rice.

When puréeing soup I would suggest that you invest in a soup emulsifier, which you can buy in any gourmet kitchen shop. They are so easy to use and they do the job of making a soup smooth. For a great texture to your soup, purée half of the ingredients and put it back into the pot.

Don't be afraid of adding cream or white/red wine to your soup! It can really enhance the flavor. If you have heart health issues, you can use almond milk. To top off a soup, garnish with microgreens, fried shallots, a dollop of sour cream, snipped chives, or any fresh herbs.

Homemade stock is obviously the best choice for all soups, but it does take time to make. I put aside a morning to make several quarts of it at a time. Before you start this process, make sure you have all the ingredients, as you don't want to have to stop to "get one thing" at the store. My stock recipe is included in this section.

I also enjoy collecting different soup bowls and quickly realized that everything does <u>NOT</u> need to match!

African Sweet Potato Soup

SERVES: 8

½ stick butter

2 tablespoons olive oil

¼ cup brown sugar

4 large sweet potatoes (peeled & sliced)

2 russet potatoes (peeled & sliced)

1 bunch celery (coarsely chopped)

1 large onion (coarsely chopped)

2 quarts good quality chicken broth

1 11-ounce can coconut milk (or more)

½ teaspoon tumeric

½ teaspoon cinnamon

2 teaspoons kosher salt & pepper

TO PREPARE:

Pre-heat oven to 350°F. Peel and cut both sweet potatoes and russet potatoes into medium slices. Place on a half sheet pan. Sprinkle brown sugar and rock salt over potatoes, and drizzle with olive oil. Roast for 25 minutes or longer until soft.

Meanwhile, add onions and celery to a large pot with butter and olive oil. Add cooked sweet potatoes and russet potatoes to the mixture. Pour in chicken broth and cook at medium heat for 25 minutes.

Add coconut milk, herbs, and spices. Purée with an emulsifier or food processor. If soup is too thick, add more chicken stock. Salt and pepper to taste. Serve hot.

Norey's Note:

Sweet potato is known as one of the "super foods", and this recipe is just wonderful.

Black Bean Soup with Beer & Spices

SERVES: 8

¼ cup olive oil

1 large onion (chopped)

3 carrots (shredded)

4 cans black beans (drained & rinsed)

5 cloves of garlic (chopped)

2 ½ quarts good quality chicken broth

1 bottle good Mexican beer

1 or 2 tablespoons balsamic vinegar

1 teaspoon sour cream per bowl (garnish)

2 bunches cilantro (chopped)

1 tablespoon kosher salt & pepper

2 tablespoons scallions (sliced for garnish)

TO PREPARE:

In a large pot, sauté onion, garlic, and carrots in olive oil on medium heat until soft. Add beans, chicken broth, and beer. Reduce heat to low and simmer for 90 minutes or until beans are soft. (Add more chicken broth as necessary.)

When beans are totally soft, add vinegar and half of the cilantro. Remove half of soup and purée with a soup emulsifier or blender. Put puréed soup back into pot and mix with original soup. Pour into bowls and and top each with a dollop of sour cream, scallions, and remaining cilantro. *P.S. This soup is also delicious with a splash of Port to finish!*

Norey's Note:

A hearty winter soup with lots of spicy flavor. It's especially popular for football tailgating!

If you want a spicier soup, add 1 or 2 cooked jalapeño chilis! Make sure they are seeded and finely chopped, then sauté for a few minutes before mixing in.

Brandied Chestnut Soup with Apples

SERVES: 8

Norey's Note:

A perfect elegant soup for Christmas holidays. It is rich, so put into <u>small</u> bowls.

This soup is really tasty!

½ stick butter

1 large onion (sliced)

3 carrots (peeled & sliced)

1 large potato (peeled & sliced)

3 celery stalks (peeled & sliced)

5 cups chicken broth

1 or 2 tablespoons good quality brandy

2 honeycrisp apples (peeled & chopped)

½ teaspoon cinnamon

2 cups chestnuts (vacuum-packed)

¼ teaspoon nutmeg

1 cup whipping cream

1 teaspoon kosher salt & pepper

TO PREPARE:

Melt butter in a large saucepan on medium heat. Add potatoes, celery, onion, carrots, and apples, and cook for 10 minutes. Add broth and chestnuts and cook for 30 minutes, stirring occasionally. Purée soup with a soup emulsifier or blender and return to pot. Add cream, nutmeg, cinnamon, salt, pepper, and brandy. Stir until reheated.

This soup is delicious served with baked saltine crackers or baked pita bread!

SOUPS

SOUPS

Cold Carrot Soup with Honey & Ginger

SERVES: 8

2 lbs carrots (peeled & shredded)

1 large onion (chopped)

6 stems celery (chopped)

3 medium potatoes (peeled & chopped)

2 quarts good quality chicken broth

1 cup whipping cream

1 tablespoon fresh ginger (chopped)

1 tablespoon good quality honey

1 tablespoon kosher salt and pepper

1 stick butter

Norey's Note:

Serve with grilled pita bread. So perfect for a hot summer dinner!

TO PREPARE:

Melt butter in a large pot. Add onions and celery, and cook until translucent. Peel carrots and potatoes and add to the pot at low temperature for five minutes. Slowly add the chicken broth. Cook until the vegetables are soft, then add the chopped ginger, honey, salt, and pepper.

Remove from stove and purée with a blender. Add cream. If the soup is too thick, add more chicken broth. This soup should be very smooth. Put it in the icebox for several hours until cold. Garnish with chopped chives just before serving.

Clam Chowder

SERVES: 8

½ stick butter

2 cloves garlic (minced)

2 large onions (chopped)

1 bunch celery (chopped)

2 cups small potatoes (cubed)

1 pound bacon (cooked crisp, chopped)

1 28-ounce can chopped clams

1 bottle clam juice

2 cups chicken broth

2 cups heavy cream

½ tablespoon water

(optional) 2 tablespoons flour

1 tablespoon <u>fresh</u> dill (fresh is a must!)

1 tablespoon kosher salt & pepper

TO PREPARE:

Put butter, onions, celery, small potato cubes, and garlic into a large pot and sauté at medium heat for 5 minutes or until soft. Add chicken broth, clam juice, and clams, and cook for 10 minutes. Add the crispy bacon and cream. Reduce heat to simmer and cook for 30 minutes.

Combine the flour and water, and slowly add to soup until it reached your desired consistency. When ready to serve, chop dill and use as a garnish over the finished soup.

P.S. You don't *have* to put flour in the soup — it is only needed if you like a thicker soup!

Norey's Note:

I'm not a big seafood eater, but even I love this soup!

I like to make it a day ahead, as it tastes even better when allowed to sit for a day.

Corn Chowder (My Way!)

SERVES: 8

½ stick butter

1 pound bacon (chopped)

2 cups onion (chopped)

2 cups celery (chopped)

2 cobs fresh corn

2 14-ounce cans creamed corn

1 cup red pepper (diced)

(optional) 2 jalapeños (seeded & chopped)

3 cups potatoes (peeled & cubed)

2 quarts good quality chicken broth (or more)

2 cups shredded sharp cheddar cheese

2 cups heavy cream

5 tablespoons fresh cilantro

5 tablespoons fresh parsley

1 teaspoon kosher salt & pepper

TO PREPARE:

In a large pot, cook onions, red peppers, celery, butter, and jalapeños (optional) on medium heat about 5 minutes or until tender. Cook bacon in another pan until crisp. Chop into pieces and set aside, leaving any remaining bacon fat in the pan. Cut corn off the cob and add to the pan of bacon fat and sauté until caramelized. Add creamed corn and chicken broth to large pot.

Add cubed potatoes, cooked corn, and cream to the pot. Cook on medium heat for 25 minutes or until potatoes are tender. Season with salt and pepper. Add the cheddar cheese and garnish with the fresh cilantro. Serve piping hot!

Norey's Note:

This soup is a delicious and hearty chowder, especially for winter. You can experiment with many different ingredients to find your perfect combination.

My favorite secret ingredient is a few finely chopped jalapeño peppers!

Cream of Tomato Soup

SERVES: 8

3 tablespoons olive oil

2 onions (coarsely chopped)

4 stalks celery (coarsely chopped)

5 cloves garlic (chopped)

2 28-ounce cans plum tomatoes in juice

3 medium russet potatoes (peeled & cubed)

1 ½ quarts chicken broth (or vegetable, good quality)

1 cup cream

1 cup fresh basil (chopped)

1 teaspoon sugar

1 teaspoon oregano

1 teaspoon sea salt & pepper

Norey's Note:

I love to serve this soup with grilled cheese sandwiches cut into quarters. Arrange the mini sandwiches around the edge of each soup plate.

You can also cut grilled cheese sandwiches into small wedges and serve with this, like tiny croutons!

TO PREPARE:

Preheat oven to 350°F and bake potatoes for 40 minutes or until softened. Put olive oil, onions, celery, and garlic in a large pot over medium heat and sauté until soft. To the pot, add canned tomatoes, chicken broth, cooked potatoes, sugar, oregano, salt, and pepper, and cook at low heat for 30 minutes. Add cream to thicken as desired. If too thick, add more chicken broth.

Purée in a blender or emulsifier until desired consistency is reached. You don't have to totally blend it, having some chunks is good as well. Garnish the finished soup with chopped fresh basil. Absolutely delicious!

SOUPS

Fresh French Lentil Soup (My Way!)

SERVES: 8

Norey's Note:

This green lentil soup is hearty and has a kick to it! Great for a fall evening with a few pieces of grilled ciabatta bread and butter.

1 package green lentils

5 cloves garlic (chopped)

1 large onion (chopped)

2 large carrots (peeled & sliced)

2 tablespoons balsamic vinegar

2 quarts chicken broth

1 bottle of beer

1 tablespoon kosher salt and pepper

1 tablespoon olive oil

1 bunch cilantro (chopped)

1 cup sour cream

TO PREPARE:

Soak the lentils in cold water overnight, then drain and set aside.

Meanwhile, add a drizzle of olive oil to a pan and sauté the chopped garlic, onions, and carrots for 10 minutes. Add the lentils and chicken broth, and cook until ingredients are soft. Put half of the soup mixture into a blender or emulsifier and blend until smooth, then pour back into remaining soup. Stir in the balsamic vinegar and cilantro, then add salt and pepper to taste. Garnish with a dollop of sour cream or a drizzle of olive oil and serve.

Fresh Mint, Avocado & Baby Pea Soup

SERVES: 8

½ stick butter

1 lemon (zested & juiced)

2 avocados (sliced)

3 large leeks (white part only, sliced)

2 russet potatoes (peeled & sliced)

2 10-ounce packages frozen baby peas

2 quarts good quality chicken broth

½ cup sour cream

1 cup fresh mint (stems removed)

1 teaspoon kosher salt & pepper

TO PREPARE:

Melt butter in a medium pot. Add leeks and cook until tender. Add the peeled potato slices and chicken broth. Cook until potatoes are soft. Add zest and juice from the lemon, salt, and pepper to the pot.

Add avocados and turn off the heat to let cool. When cool, add frozen peas and most of the fresh mint. Purée in a blender or emulsifier until desired consistency is reached. Serve with baked saltine crackers and a dollop of sour cream on top. Garnish with a sprig of fresh mint.

Norey's Note:

The fresh mint is the key ingredient.

It is important <u>NOT</u> to put the peas into the soup until the end, as you want the "green" to be vibrant. It is a very easy soup to make.

Greek Vegetable Soup

SERVES: 8

- 3 tablespoons olive oil
- 2 fresh lemons (zested & juiced)
- 2 large onions (sliced)
- 4 garlic cloves (or more, chopped)
- 4 carrots (peeled and sliced)
- 4 celery stalks (peeled and sliced)
- 1 red pepper (diced)
- 1 jar artichoke hearts (drained & sliced into quarters)
- 1 9-ounce can diced tomatoes (drained)
- 1 cup arugula (stems removed and lightly chopped)
- 2 quarts chicken broth (preferably homemade)
- ½ cup hummus (preferably homemade)
- 3 or 4 tablespoons fresh mint
- 1 teaspoon fresh thyme
- 1 tablespoon kosher salt and pepper (or more)
- (optional) 1 cup feta cheese (crumbled)

Norey's Note:

This soup is extra delicious when served with a sprinkle of feta cheese on top!

TO PREPARE:

In a large saucepan, sauté onions and garlic in olive oil on medium heat until tender and fragrant. Add celery, red peppers, and carrots and cook for 5 minutes. Stir in chicken broth, tomatoes, lemon juice, and lemon zest. Add hummus spread. Increase heat to high and bring mixture to a boil for 5 minutes, stirring constantly.

Heat olive oil in a frying pan. Cook artichokes without stirring until browned on one side. Medium dice the cooked artichokes and add to soup. Deglaze pan with ¼ cup stock. Transfer 1 cup of soup to a blender and purée it. Pour back into remaining soup. Chop mint, arugula, and fresh thyme for a garnish, season with salt and pepper, and serve.

SOUPS

Jellied White Gazpacho

SERVES: 4

½ cup celery (finely chopped)

½ cup English cucumber (finely chopped)

2 tablespoons red onion (finely chopped)

12 cherry tomatoes (seeded & coarsely chopped)

1 ½ packages Knox® gelatin

1 ½ cups cold water (separated)

2 cups chicken broth (preferably homemade)

½ cup white vinegar

½ teaspoon hot sauce

½ teaspoon paprika

½ teaspoon fresh basil (chopped)

½ teaspoon fresh thyme

1 teaspoon kosher salt

fresh chives (snipped, for garnish)

TO PREPARE:

In a small bowl, sprinkle Knox® gelatin over ½ cup cold water. Add chicken broth and place over low heat, stirring constantly for about 3 minutes or until gelatin dissolves. Add vinegar, salt, paprika, basil, thyme, and hot sauce. Remove from heat. Chill in refrigerator until mixture has the consistency of <u>stiff</u> egg whites.

Fold in chopped celery, cucumber, onions, and tomatoes. Chill again for at least 3 hours; it will be jelly-like when ready. Cut into bite-size squares or spoon into small bowls. Garnish with fresh snipped chives and serve with hot, crusty bread of your choice.

Norey's Note:

A pretty spring soup. Serve in a glass bowl or clear cup so you can see the jelly!

This soup needs a <u>rich</u> chicken broth for best results.

Mushroom Bisque with Port

SERVES: 8

3 tablespoons butter

1 large onion (chopped)

4 stalks celery (chopped)

2 pounds white mushrooms (chopped)

2 large portobello mushrooms (chopped)

2 medium potatoes (peeled and chopped)

2 quarts chicken broth (or more)

1 cup cream

(optional) 2 tablespoons Port wine

1 teaspoon kosher salt & pepper

Norey's Note:

This is a wonderful soup for a winter dinner. The Port is only an add-on if one likes it. It does give it a zip!

TO PREPARE:

Sauté onions and celery in a large pot on medium heat until translucent, then set aside. Add mushrooms and sauté for 5 minutes until well cooked and any water from the mushrooms has dissolved, as it gives the soup a better flavor.

Add the peeled potatoes and continue to cook (about five minutes). Add the chicken broth. Reduce heat to low and let cook for 20 minutes. Stir in cream and cook for 1 more minute.

Use a blender or purée in batches in a food processor until smooth. Thin mixture down with chicken broth if it is too thick. Drizzle Port wine on top if desired. If you prefer a different garnish, try a dollop of sour cream!

Roasted Butternut Squash & Apple Soup

SERVES: 8–10

¼ cup virgin olive oil

2 large leeks (rinsed and sliced)

2 large honeycrisp apples (peeled & sliced)

3 medium russet potatoes (sliced)

¼ cup brown sugar

4 stalks celery (chopped)

2 small butternut squashes (peeled & sliced)

2 quarts good quality chicken broth (or more)

1 cup fresh apple cider

1 teaspoon kosher salt & pepper

TO PREPARE:

Place butternut squash and sliced potatoes on a half sheet pan. Sprinkle with olive oil, brown sugar, and kosher salt. Roast at 400°F for 20 minutes or until golden brown. Remove pan from oven. Sauté leeks and celery in a large pot for 5 minutes. Add the roasted butternut squash, potoatoes, chicken broth, cider, and apple slices to the pot and cook on medium heat until potatoes are soft.

Use a blender or food processor to purée until smooth. Add salt and pepper to taste. Serve immediately.

Optional Garnish: Take an extra 2 small apples and shred with a grater. Sauté in ½ teaspoon olive oil until golden brown and caramelized. Add 1 teaspoon sugar and combine well. Sprinkle mixture on top of finished soup as a garnish.

Norey's Note:

Perfect for a fall supper. Make this soup with a hearty salad, plus your favorite warm bread, and you have a complete meal!

SOUPS

Roasted Cauliflower & Apple Soup

SERVES: 8

½ stick butter
2 tablespoons olive oil
1 Vidalia onion (chopped)
1 cup celery (chopped)
2 large russet potatoes (peeled & chopped)
2 honeycrisp apples (peeled & chopped)
2 small cauliflower (broken into small florets)
2 quarts good quality chicken broth
(optional) ½ cup apple cider
½ cup light cream
1 tablespoon kosher salt & pepper
(optional) ½ teaspoon curry

Norey's Note:

Cauliflower has a wonderful nutty flavor. When people taste this soup there is always an "ahh!" from their lips... And then someone always asks for the recipe!

This soup can be made a day ahead of your meal, and you can substitute vegetable broth for chicken broth if you wish!

TO PREPARE:

In a large pot, cook onions and celery in butter until tender. Toss cauliflower in 2 tablespoons of olive oil and place on a half-sheet pan. Sprinkle a bit of kosher salt on top and bake at 400°F for 15 minutes. *Do not burn cauliflower!*

Meanwhile, add chopped potatoes and apples to the pot. Pour the chicken broth and apple cider into pot and cook until tender. When the cauliflower has caramelized, add to pot as well. Add light cream and a pinch of curry powder (if desired). Salt and pepper to taste and run the mixture through a blender or emulsifier until smooth. Top with grated apple or fresh chopped chives!

Roasted Red Pepper & Tomato Soup

SERVES: 8

3 tablespoons extra virgin olive oil

1 64-ounce can plum tomatoes

3 red peppers (roasted)

2 onions (coarsely chopped)

2 medium russet potatoes (peeled & sliced)

5 garlic cloves (chopped)

2 quarts quality chicken broth

1 tablespoon sugar

1 teaspoon oregano

10 <u>fresh</u> basil leaves (chopped)

2 teaspoons kosher salt & pepper

Norey's Note:

It is a must to use <u>fresh</u> basil!

I love the combination of roasted red peppers and tomatoes. It is just a great flavor, especially when you add chopped basil to it.

TO PREPARE:

<u>Red peppers:</u> If you have a gas stove, carefully put peppers right over flame until blackened, turning every few minutes. Otherwise, cut peppers in half and toss with olive oil to coat, then roast at 400°F for 15 minutes. When cool, the skin should come right off.

Add onions, celery, and garlic to a large pot with olive oil and sauté 5–6 minutes until tender. Add tomatoes, peeled red peppers, potatoes, sugar, oregano, and broth, and cook for 20 minutes over medium heat. Once potatoes are soft, remove pot from heat and run mixture through a blender until smooth. Salt and pepper to taste. Mix in most of the chopped basil. Garnish with remaining chopped basil and serve with hot, crusty ciabatta bread with butter.

SOUPS

SALADS

Salads

I could eat salads for breakfast, lunch, and dinner! There are so many varieties of lettuce to choose from today. If possible, I try to get to the local farmer's market and buy lettuce that was just picked that day. I realize not everyone has access to farmer's markets, but there is nothing better. The joy of picking out different fresh lettuces makes my mouth water as I write!

Lettuce usually has remnants of the earth on it so make sure you wash it well. I get a large bowl and rip the lettuce leaves before adding to cold water. Swish the lettuce around with your hands and then wrap in paper towels. Don't toss the lettuce too many times as it may wilt. If you have a lettuce spinner, use that first, then into the icebox it goes.

Garden tomatoes of any shape or size are king of the summer garden! There is NOTHING better than a slice of tomato with a piece of basil right out of the garden. I <u>never</u> put my tomatoes in the icebox, as they get watery and lose their texture. Tomatoes can stand on their own, but a BLT takes on a new meaning during tomato season. Roasting plum tomatoes is special too, as they become super sweet and can be added to just about any appetizer, especially bruschetta.

Almost any vegetable can go on the grill with a brush of olive oil and rock salt. I like to add hot grilled vegetables to a salad at the end and toss. Great contrast of cold lettuce and hot vegetables! Onions are *so good* grilled. Many people can't eat raw onions, so grilling them solves that problem.

<u>A list of possibilities for salads:</u> Grilled corn cut off the cob, any type of onion, peas, asparagus, eggplant, blueberries, cranberries, strawberries, watermelon, kiwi, red grapes, golden raisins, toasted almonds, pecans... ANY fresh herbs also make a huge difference!

There are so many different dressing for salads too. If the lettuce is super fresh, I just use olive oil and a squeeze of lemon, or several drops of balsamic. A bit of crumbled cheese on top always works for me! I like feta, bleu cheese, goat cheese, or fresh grated parmesan.

Arugula & Pomegranate Salad

SERVES: 8

SALADS

½ teapoon olive oil
1 cup almonds (sliced)
½ cup vegetable oil
1 pomegranate (seeded)
2 bunches baby arugula
2 carrots (peeled and sliced)
2 hard-boiled eggs (sliced)

1 cup parmesan cheese (grated)
1 teaspoon dijon mustard
3 tablespoons white vinegar
3 tablespoons olive oil
1 tablespoon sugar
kosher salt and pepper

TO PREPARE:

In a frying pan, sauté almonds in olive oil over medium heat for 2 minutes, <u>carefully watching</u> so they don't burn. Sprinkle with salt and set aside.

Seed the pomegranate and shave the parmesan cheese. Using a peeler, make long, thin slices of the carrots.

Mix all remaining liquid ingredients in a small jar, shaking until well blended. Toss arugula with desired amount of dressing. Layer ingredients starting with dressed baby arugula, then carrots, then sliced egg, then shaved parmesan. Top with toasted almonds and pomegranate, and drizzle with additional dressing as needed.

Norey's Note:

This is a delicious, healthy, and pretty salad. It is one of my very favorites. The toasted almonds add a wonderful crunch; adding any kind of salted nuts is always good!

Bib & Boston Salad with Bleu Cheese & Almonds

SERVES: 4

cooking spray

1 head bib lettuce

1 head Boston lettuce

1 bunch red grapes

½ cup sliced almonds

1 or 2 avocados (sliced)

½ cup Maytag® bleu cheese (crumbled)

(optional) ½ cup golden raisins

2 tablespoons fresh chives (chopped)

2 tablespoons fresh parsley (chopped)

small amount of sea salt and pepper

Norey's Note:

A pretty salad with lots of healthy ingredients!

TO PREPARE:

Wash lettuces and wrap in a paper towel. Refrigerate for a few hours to chill. Sauté almonds in a frying pan sprayed with cooking spray. <u>Watch almonds carefully as they can burn quickly.</u> Remove from heat as they start to brown and toss with a little sea salt. Set aside.

Arrange chilled lettuce on plates and add 3–4 slices of avocado. Add the toasted almonds, grapes, and crumbled cheese, then top with fresh chives. and parsley.

Drizzle either Honey Lemon Vinaigrette (pg. 137) or Sweet Balsamic Dressing (pg. 139) over finished salad. Serve with toasted pita.

SALADS

Chopped Baby Kale Salad with Avocado

SERVES: 4

1 bunch arugula

1 package <u>baby</u> kale (washed carefully & chopped)

1 avocado (sliced)

1 large carrot (peeled & sliced thin)

(optional) 2 eggs

½ cup fresh parmesan cheese (or more, sliced thin)

Dressing:

½ cup olive oil

1 large garlic clove (minced)

¼ cup white balsamic vinegar

1 teaspoon sugar

kosher salt & pepper

TO PREPARE:

If using eggs, hard-boil eggs in boiling water for 10–12 minutes, then rinse under cold water. Peel immediately, slice thinly or cut into quarters, and add on top of kale.

Toss the arugula and kale together with sliced avocado and carrots, and add to salad platter. Top with parmesan cheese.

Mix olive oil, garlic, vinegar, sugar, and salt together to create dressing. Salt and pepper to taste, then drizzle dressing over the salad. Serve immediately.

Norey's Note:

This is a healthy salad I developed while trying to eat better. It is both filling and pleasing to look at!

If you don't like kale, you can substitute any type of lettuce you wish.

SALADS

Chopped Kitchen Sink Salad

SERVES: 8

Norey's Note:

Get creative—Use whatever you have in your icebox! You also don't have to use all these ingredients... choose the ones you like!

This salad was one of the most popular items in my restaurant; customers couldn't wait to see what would be in the salad each week.

deli meat (your choice; cubed)

1 large head of lettuce (your choice)

1 red bell pepper (sliced)

2 boxes of cherry tomatoes (in season, quartered)

1 red onion (sliced)

1 scallion (sliced)

1 English cucumber (sliced)

2 carrots (shredded & sliced)

2 avocados (sliced)

a few slices of ham or chicken

dried cranberries

golden raisins

black beans (washed)

chickpeas (drained)

deli cheeses (your choice: bleu, feta, goat, cheddar...)

2 eggs (hard-boiled)

nuts (your choice, toasted)

parsley

chives

basil

TO PREPARE:

Chop ingredients into bite-size pieces and combine in a large bowl. <u>Do not use a food processor for this salad</u> as it will get too mushy. I like to toss this salad with 1000 Island Dressing (pg. 136) or Honey Lemon Vinaigrette (pg. 137). Serve immediately with a slice of hot, crusty bread.

SALADS

Chopped Wedge Salad with Arugula & Bleu Cheese

SERVES: 8

1 pound bacon (cooked crisp and broken into pieces)

2 heads romaine lettuce (chopped)

1 bunch baby arugula (chopped)

½ box sweet yellow tomatoes (halved)

½ box red cherry tomatoes (halved)

2 avocados (sliced)

1 shallot (sliced)

2 tablespoons fresh snipped chives

Dressing:

½ cup Hellmann's® mayonnaise

½ cup sour cream

1 tablespoon Worchestershire sauce

2 tablespoons white wine vinegar

3 oz good quality bleu cheese (crumbled)

kosher salt and pepper

TO PREPARE:

Heat a thin layer of oil in a frying pan. Dust sliced shallots with flour and add to pan, frying until crisp. Set aside. Cook bacon until crisp and drain on a paper towel. Sauté yellow and red tomatoes in a drizzle of olive oil for 4 or 5 minutes.

Mix mayonnaise, sour cream, Worchestershire sauce, vinegar, and bleu cheese together with salt and pepper to make the dressing. Toss lettuces in dressing and arrange on a plate. Top with tomatoes, sliced avocado, crispy bacon, and fried shallots. Garnish with the snipped chives and bleu cheese.

Norey's Note:

A different take on the tranditional "wedge" salad.

Elegant Caesar Salad

SERVES: 8

½ pound cooked bacon (crispy, chopped)
2 large heads of romaine lettuce
1 pint sweet cherry tomatoes (halved)
2 avocados (sliced)
2 tablespoons olive oil
1 cup fresh parmesan cheese (sliced)

Croutons:
2 or 3 tablespoons olive oil
1 loaf French baguette or ciabatta
kosher salt and pepper

Norey's Note:

Delicious when served with my Caesar Salad Dressing on page 136!

TO PREPARE:

Wash and chop lettuce and wrap in a clean kitchen towl or paper towels. Toss tomatoes in 2 tablespoons olive oil and marinate at room temperature for 1 hour. Arrange on a small sheet pan. Sprinkle with salt and pepper, then roast at 400°F for 10 minutes.

Homemade Croutons: Cut selected bread into bite-size pieces. Toss with olive oil and roast at 400°F for 5 minutes. Watch the bread carefully so it does not burn. Toss with salt and pepper, and set aside.

Layer ingredients on a serving plate. Sprinkle with homemade croutons and serve with Caesar Salad Dressing (pg. 136). Top with sliced avocado and chopped bacon. Finish with fresh parmesan to complete this salad.

SALADS

End of Summer Salad

SERVES: 4

1 bunch baby spinach
1 bunch baby salad greens
1 bunch arugula
1 pint sweet cherry tomatoes
2 avocados (thickly sliced)
½ cup golden raisins
1 cup fresh blueberries
½ cup sliced almonds
1 cup good quality granola
(optional) ½ cup goat cheese (crumbled)
1 bunch scallions (sliced)
1 tablespoon olive oil

Dressing:
Honey Lemon Vinaigrette (pg. 137)

Norey's Note:

You can also use toasted walnuts if you like them better than almonds.

TO PREPARE:

Toss arugula and baby greens with Honey Lemon Vinaigrette (pg. 137).

Sauté cherry tomatoes in a small pan with a tablespoon of olive oil for 3–4 minutes. Set aside when done. Sauté sliced almonds in the same pan for 1 minute. <u>Watch carefully as almonds burn quickly!</u>

Portion out dressed lettuce on each plate. Add sautéed tomatoes and almonds, sliced avocado, granola, blueberries, scallions, and raisins. Top with crumbled goat cheese. Drizzle a bit more dressing on top to complete, and serve.

Grandma Benner's Salad with Hot Dressing

SERVES: 6–8

2 bunches frisée and/or baby kale

10 slices bacon

1 large egg

1 tablespoon flour

2 tablespoons mayonnaise

2 tablespoons white vinegar

1 teaspoon salt

1 tablespoon sugar

¾ cup water

Optional Serving Garnishes:

1 small red onion (sliced)

2 large eggs (hardboiled, sliced)

½ cup toasted almonds

TO PREPARE:

Cook bacon until crisp. <u>Retain half of the fat</u> left over in the pan. Mix egg, flour, mayonnaise, sugar, and salt together in a medium frying pan over medium heat. Slowly add water and vinegar. Add in leftover bacon fat and stir until dressing starts to thicken. Top frisée and/or kale with the cooked bacon and hot dressing to serve.

Optional serving suggestion: This recipe is especially delicious with the addition of sliced red onion, sliced hard boiled eggs, and almonds to your salad. Top the leafy greens with these ingredients before drizzling hot dressing.

Norey's Note:

This dressing is an old Pennsylvania Dutch recipe.

It's great over frisée and other bitter leafy greens like kale or arugula. It's also delicious in potato salad!

SALADS

SALADS

Hot Vegetable Salad with Arugula

SERVES: 6

1 larege bunch fresh arugula

1 small head cauliflower (broken into pieces)

1 small head broccoli (broken into pieces)

2 red peppers (chopped)

1 large onion (chopped)

2 zucchini (sliced)

2 carrots (peeled and sliced thin)

1 box sweet cherry tomatoes

(optional) 1 cup golden raisins

1 cup feta or shaved parmesan cheese

2 avocados (thickly sliced)

½ cup good olive oil

kosher salt and pepper

TO PREPARE:

Comine all of the vegetables (except avocados) with olive oil in a large bowl, and season with salt and pepper to taste. Toss thoroughly. Cover a half-sheet pan with aluminum foil, then arrange the vegetables on it in a single layer. Cook at 400°F for about 20 minutes, shaking the pan a few times while it cooks to get all sides crispy.

Meanwhile, sauté cherry tomatoes and raisins in a small frying pan with a few tablespoons of olive oil, and add to cooked vegetables. Toss hot vegetable mixture with arugula, and add a bit of vinegar or your favorite dressing (I like the Honey Lemon Vinaigrette on pg. 137). Finish with a garnish of feta cheese and sliced avocado.

Norey's Note:

This has become my "go-to" salad almost every night. I just love it and it is healthy and colorful.

Once again, fresh vegetables make all the difference!

SALADS

My Version of Waldorf Salad

SERVES: 6

Norey's Note:

The colors in this salad are wonderful. A beautiful and healthy luncheon dish.

2 Honeycrisp apples

1 cup red grapes (halved)

1 cup celery (sliced)

½ cup dried apricots

½ cup fresh blueberries

½ cup almonds (toasted)

½ cup cashews (toasted)

fresh mint leaves (garnish)

Dressing:

½ cup Hellmann's® mayonnaise

1 tablespoon apple cider vinegar

1 tablespoon creamy peanut butter

2 teaspoons sugar

TO PREPARE:

Cut apples into bite-size chunks (leave the skin on) and put in a large bowl. Add celery, red grapes, apricots, and blueberries. In a small bowl mix mayonnaise, vinegar, peanut butter, and sugar together until smooth to create the dressing. Toss dressing with other salad ingredients. Arrange salad in a glass bowl and top with toasted nuts. Garnish with fresh mint leaves.

Refrigerate for at least 30 minutes before serving.

SALADS

Quinoa Salad with Fresh Veggies & Feta

SERVES: 8

¼ cup olive oil (or more)

1 large lemon (juice)

1 French cucumber (peeled & chopped)

12 sweet cherry tomatoes (halved)

½ small red onion (chopped)

2 cups chicken broth (low sodium)

½ cup quinoa

1 cup feta cheese (crumbled)

1 cup fresh mint (chopped)

1 cup fresh parsley (chopped)

kosher salt & pepper

Norey's Note:

A refreshing, healthy salad into which you can add any other ingredients you enjoy, such as corn off the cob!

I like to arrange this salad in a shallow, pretty bowl lined with Boston lettuce.

TO PREPARE:

Bring chicken broth to a boil in a medium sauce pan. Add quinoa, then cover and simmer about 5 minutes until broth is absorbed. Remove from heat and let cool for about 20 minutes.

Mix all chopped vegetables and herbs together with quinoa. Add juice from lemon, olive oil, and all the chopped herbs. Salt and pepper to taste. Crumble feta cheese on top and refrigerate until ready to serve.

Roasted Butternut Squash & Arugula Salad

SERVES: 6

2 tablespoons olive oil

1 bunch baby arugula

1 head romaine lettuce (loosely chopped)

1 medium butternut squash (peeled, diced)

2 tablespoons light brown sugar

½ cup dried cranberries or golden raisins

2 ounces goat cheese (crumbled)

1 teaspoon kosher salt and pepper

Toasted Pecans:

1 egg white (whisked until frothy)

1 cup pecans

1 tablespoon sugar

½ teaspoon cayenne pepper

1 teaspoon kosher salt

TO PREPARE:

Toss squash in olive oil and arrance on a half baking sheet lined with aluminum foil. Sprinkle with brown sugar and salt. Bake at 400°F for 15 or 20 minutes, or until squash starts to caramelize. Set aside.

To toast pecans: mix egg white with brown sugar and salt. Toss pecans in egg mixture until coated, and roast on a sheet pan at 400°F for 10 minutes. Watch pecans carefully as they easily burn!

Arrange lettuce on a plate and add warm butternut squash. Top with goat cheese, pecans, and dried cranberries. Drizzle with my Sweet Balsamic Dressing (pg. 139).

Norey's Note:

This fall salad has so many great flavors in it, and it is very pretty as well!

Feel free to substitute the arugula with kale; it is just as delicious.

SANDWICHES

Sandwiches

There is nothing better to me than a "tea sandwich". They are tiny two-bite delicacies, so no one ever feels guilty about eating more than one!

My mother used to make us PB&J (peanut butter and jelly) and remove the crust which—through some miracle—made them taste so much better. Tea sandwiches are perfect for a lunch served with soup, an afternoon tea or a cocktail party. I often make a variety at my cocktail parties, and I notice that they are always the first hors d'oeuvres to go!

The following is a list of some of my favorite tea sandwich combinations. I usually make these with Pepperidge Farm® *thin-sliced* white or whole-wheat bread.

- Cream cheese and olives
- Watercress, cream cheese, and chives
- Hungarian cheese spread with thin-sliced cucumbers
- Egg salad with chives and arugula
- Chicken salad with chopped apricots and toasted almonds
- Ham salad with sweet chopped pickles or green relish (drained)
- Tuna salad with chopped celery
- Crabmeat salad with Bib lettuce
- Smoked salmon salad with cream cheese, capers, a small red onion, chopped lime, and fresh dill
- Grilled cheese, cooked bacon, and hot pepper jelly
- Meatloaf and arugula with mayo
- Bleu cheese, cream cheese, dried cranberries, and scallions
- Cucumber, scallions, and cream cheese
- Mini BLTs with avocado
- Avocado, thinly sliced tomatoes, and fresh basil
- Roast beef, brie, and horseradish sauce
- Apple, bacon, and cheddar cheese
- The Classic: PB&J
- Peanut butter and banana with Bib lettuce
- Cinnamon raisin bread with cream cheese, almonds, and dried apricots

The Art of Making a Perfect Tea Sandwich

First and foremost, the bread *must be fresh!* Always make sure to check the date on the bread. I *always* use Hellmann's® mayonnaise. I have tried everything on the market, and it is the best, unless, of course, you have the time to make your own.

Always have any cream cheese out at room temperature so it is soft.

When you make the sandwich filling, put all the ingredients together and let the flavors "sit" for at least an hour. The tea sandwiches should be assembled at the last minute, so have all the ingredients, bread, etc. organized and lined up so you can create an assembly line.

Cut thin bread on a cutting board. Make sure you spread the ingredients to the very <u>end</u> of the slice so every bite is good! I always put a small dab of mayo on one side so the ingredients stick to the bread and it holds the sandwich together.

Remove crusts on all four sides. Cut diagonally corner-to-corner into four triangles with a serrated knife. Place sandwiches standing up on a short side on a pretty platter with a white paper doily on the bottom.

If offering a range of sandwich types, keep them separated so everyone knows which sandwiches are which. Placecards can also be used to label each sandwich type. If it is summertime, garnish with a sprig of fresh thyme or mint

To keep sandwiches fresh, wet a paper towel and squeeze out any excess moisture. Place on top of sandwiches and cover the entire platter with plastic wrap. Garnish your platters with fresh dill, parsley, or a few pretty flowers such as nasturtiums.

Sandwiches can stay at room temperature for up to an hour. Refrigerate if it will be more than an hour between prep and serving!

SANDWICHES

Cinnamon Raisin Bread with Cream Cheese & Chutney

SERVES: 6

1 loaf cinnamon raisin bread (I like Pepperidge Farm®)

1 8-ounce package cream cheese (softened)

3 tablespoons chutney

1 tablespoon chives (chopped)

Norey's Note:

This is a delicious tea sandwich that looks great arranged on a plate with other types of small sandwiches!

TO PREPARE:

Mix chutney with cream cheese and chives. Spread a good amount between two slices of bread. Cut off the crusts and slice into triangles. Very easy, and very delicious!

SANDWICHES

Day After Thanksgiving Sandwich

SERVES: 6

Norey's Note:

This is my all-time favorite sandwich. I can't wait for the day <u>after</u> Thanksgiving, just so I can make this sandwich!

½ fresh turkey breast (approx. 1lb., sliced)

1 head Boston lettuce

½ cup Hellmann's® mayonnaise

2 cups homemade stuffing

1 can jellied cranberry sauce

1 loaf bread or soft rolls (any kind, toasted)

kosher salt and pepper

(optional) ½ pound bacon (cooked crisp)

TO PREPARE:

To make stuffing (if you don't have leftovers!), buy your favorite stovetop stuffing mix and add in some sautéed onions and celery. You can also make your own version from scratch.

Spread mayonnaise on the inside of two slices of bread. I prefer white bread, but whole wheat is also good. Add turkey to each side. Place a good amount of stuffing on one side and top with a layer of cranberry sauce. Add lettuce to the other side. Fold together and cut in half. You may want to use toothpicks to hold everything together while you cut!

As an addition, you may want to add a slice of cooked bacon on the lettuce side for a bit more of a salty crunch.

Egg Salad Sandwich with Bacon, Arugula & Tomato

SERVES: 6

- 8 slices bacon (cooked crisp)
- 1 small bunch baby arugula
- 2 ripe tomatoes, in season (sliced)
- 8 large eggs
- 1 loaf bread of your choice
- 3 tablespoons mayonnaise
- 1 teaspoon sweet mustard
- 12 chives (snipped)
- kosher salt & pepper

TO PREPARE:

Boil eggs in a medium-sized pot for 12 minutes and then rinse under cold water to remove shells easily. Roughly chop eggs to your desired size, then mix in mustard, mayonnaise, and snipped chives. Thinly slice tomatoes and drain on a paper towel as well. Toast bread lightly if desired.

Cut crusts off bread and assemble each sandwich by spreading mayonnaise on the inside of two pieces of bread. Add arugula to one side and a mound of egg salad to the other. Add tomato and cooked bacon to one side. Fold bread together and slice in half.

Norey's Note:

Make sure to get <u>fresh</u> seasonal tomatoes, it makes a huge difference!

SANDWICHES

Goat Cheese & Tomato Sandwiches

SERVES: 8

8 sundried tomatoes (drained)
2 large ripe tomatoes, seasonal (sliced)
1 small red onion (thinly sliced)
8 ounces goat cheese (softened)
1 loaf ciabatta bread (thinly sliced)
16 large basil leaves (sliced)
kosher salt and pepper
(optional) 1 head Boston lettuce

TO PREPARE:

Combine goat cheese and sundried tomatoes in a food processor and pulse just a few times. Drain fresh tomato slices on a paper towel. Put bread under oven broiler for 30 seconds just to lightly toast.

Put a good amount of goat cheese on the inside of each slice of bread. Layer sliced tomatoes, fresh basil, onion, and lettuce (optional) on one slice of bread, then sprinkle with salt and pepper. Top with a second slice of bread. Cut in half and serve.

Grilled Peanut Butter & Jelly

SERVES: 4

1 teaspoon butter (per sandwich)

1 package Syrian bread (thin)

1 cup peanut butter (any kind)

1 cup strawberry or blueberry preserves

TO PREPARE:

Slice Syrian bread in half so that you have two round pieces. Put peanut butter on one side and preserves on the other. Fold the pieces of bread together.

Place butter in a frying pan and allow butter to melt. When pan is hot, put the sandwich in and cook for 1 minute. Turn over and cook for another minute. Continue flipping until bread is golden-brown on both sides. Remove from pan, let cool, then slice in half.

Norey's Note:

Add sliced bananas for an extra twist!

You can also cut these sandwiches into quarters and serve as an appetizer.

This PB&J is simple BUT divine!

SANDWICHES

Smoked Salmon Sandwich

SERVES: 6

8 ounces good quality smoked salmon

1 small red onion (thinly sliced)

1 head Boston lettuce

2 large eggs (hard boiled and sliced)

1 loaf pumpernickel or seeded rye bread

8 ounces cream cheese (softened)

2 tablespoons capers

TO PREPARE:

Spread softened cream cheese on both slices of bread. Assemble in the following order: smoked salmon, slices of hard boiled egg, red onion, capers, and lettuce. Cut in halves or quarters.

Norey's Note:

Pretty and delicious!

SANDWICHES

Entrées

The world of food has changed so much in the past decade, especially entrées! Now there are vegetarians, vegans, pescatarians, et cetera. I'm often asked if I should provide a separate dish if an individual has allergies or diet restrictions. The answer to myself is yes, of course. I have tried to create a special menu for some of my guests, but that can get tedious if there are several!! I do try to be positively responsive, so if I know in advance, I normally will produce a vegetable dish for that person (see my vegetable section, beginning on page 125).

I usually choose my entrée first, and then work backwards and build the rest of the menu accordingly. Dinner-size salads, hearty soups, breads, and a variety of vegetables can also count for a "main meal". Once I choose the menu, I can then begin to set the table with appropriate table and glassware.

Colors of food mean something to me, so I try to compliment the entrée with colorful accompaniments. Make sure that you have the correct utensils for steaks, fish, and chicken. Obviously, I like to cook according to each season, so vegetables, grilling out, fresh local seafood (even though I do NOT eat seafood!) become very important. If you grill the meat of your main meal, make sure to leave a good 15 minutes so the entrée can "rest" and the juices remain in the meat.

Chicken Florentine

SERVES: 4

First layer:

3 packages frozen leaf spinach (drained well)

2 tablespoons butter (melted)

2 tablespoons olive oil

1 onion (chopped)

2 cloves garlic (chopped)

1 tablespoon flour

½ cup chicken broth (or more)

½ cup light cream

Second layer:

1 large package boneless chicken breast tenders

1 stick butter

1 tablespoon flour

½ cup cream

1 ½ cup chicken broth (or more)

1 cup parmesan cheese

salt and pepper

TO PREPARE:

Preheat oven to 400°F. For the first layer, thaw spinach and squeeze the liquid out with your hands. Sauté onion and garlic, then mix in flour and butter to make a roux. Add spinach and cook for about 5 minutes. Put chicken on a half sheet pan and sprinkle with olive oil, salt, and pepper. Cover with aluminum and bake 15 minutes. Slice when cooled and set aside.

Spray a 9"x13" casserole dish. Layer first with spinach mixture, then arrange a second layer of sliced chicken pieces on top.

To finish the "second layer", add butter, flour, cream, and broth to a pan and mix over medium heat. Pour the cream sauce over the chicken and sprinkle with parmesan. Bake for 20 minutes or until it bubbles.

Norey's Note:

A wonderful entrée to prepare ahead for a party. It freezes well and is delicious!

I love to sauté halved artichokes in a bit of butter until golden, then serve on top of this chicken.

This recipe is also delicious served with a clean salad and hot rolls.

Chicken Marsala with Mushrooms, Capers & Leeks

SERVES: 6

3 boneless chicken breasts (cut in half)

¼ cup olive oil

1 cup bread crumbs

½ stick butter

3 large leeks (white part only, washed and sliced)

2 pounds small white mushrooms (sliced)

1 cup chicken broth (or more)

¼ to ½ cup Marsala wine

(optional) ¼ cup capers (drained and chopped)

(optional) ½ cup parsley (chopped)

1 tablespoon salt and pepper

Norey's Note:

The chicken should be as thin as possible, so be patient when pounding it down.

You can also use wax paper or ziplock bags to pound chicken if you don't have parchment paper handy.

TO PREPARE:

With a mallet, pound chicken between two sheets of parchment paper or in a ziplock bag until ¼-inch thin. Season the breadcrumbs with salt and pepper. Heat oil in a large sauté pan over high heat. Cover chicken with seasoned bread crumbs and sauté in batches about 1 minute each side or until cooked through, adding more oil as necessary. Set aside.

Melt butter in the pan and keep heat on high. Add mushrooms and leeks and sauté until soft and translucent. Cook until mushrooms have given off <u>all</u> their moisture. Add Marsala wine and cook until slightly reduced in volume. Add chicken broth, stirring until hot. Pour sauce over cooked chicken. Garnish with parsley and capers if you like.

Chicken Paillard with Grilled Lemon Artichokes

SERVES: 6

4 boneless chicken breasts

½ cup flour (seasoned with salt and pepper)

2 jars artichoke hearts (or frozen)

1 tablespoon olive oil (for artichokes)

2 tablespoons butter

¼ cup vegetable oil

1 lemon (squeezed and zested)

1 tablespoon Dijon mustard

½ cup heavy cream

½ cup chicken broth (or more as needed)

1 teaspoon kosher salt & pepper

TO PREPARE:

Pound chicken breasts between two pieces of parchment paper with a mallet until they are about ½ inch thick. Lightly coat each piece of chicken with seasoned flour. Heat a little oil in a large sauté pan over medium heat. When oil is hot, add 2 pieces of chicken. Cook for 2 minutes, flipping once, until golden brown. Set aside and cook the other 2 pieces of chicken the same way.

Sprinkle olive oil, lemon juice, and salt on the artichokes and put under broiler until golden, <u>making sure you watch them so they don't burn!</u>

Bring butter, lemon, and chicken broth to a boil in a medium sauce pan. Add mustard and cream. Stir well and cook until slightly thickened. Season with salt and pepper. If needed, place all 4 chicken breasts on a sheet pan in the oven at 300°F for 10 minutes to warm. Place grilled artichokes on top of chicken. Pour sauce over top and serve.

Norey's Note:

The grilled artichoke hearts add special flavor to this dish.

It's especially delicious when served over or with your favorite rice!

ENTRÉES

ENTRÉES

Chicken Pot Pie My Way

SERVES: 6–8

4 chicken breasts

1 stick butter (melted)

olive oil (to taste)

1 large onion (chopped medium)

1 cup celery (diced)

4 large cloves garlic (chopped fine)

2 cups carrots (sliced)

1 cup broccoli (cut into <u>small</u> pieces)

1 box frozen baby peas

2 cups small white mushrooms (sliced)

2 cups chicken broth (good quality)

½ to 1 cup medium cream

2 tablespoons flour

1 cup fresh parsley and basil (mixed)

2 teaspoons salt & pepper

store-bought puff pastry
    (I like Pepperidge Farm®)

1 egg

(optional) 1 cup parmesan cheese

TO PREPARE:

Put chicken breasts on a sheet pan and sprinkle with oil, salt, and pepper. Cover with aluminum foil and bake at 375°F for 20 minutes or until they are done. Let sit for a few minutes and cut into bite-sized pieces. Set aside.

Melt butter in a large pan and add garlic, onions, and celery. Sauté until translucent, about 5 minutes, and set aside. Sauté sliced mushrooms in a tablespoon of butter and cook until moisture is gone and mushrooms start to get golden. Add to prepared onion mixture. Put carrots in a small amount of water and boil until tender, then do the same with broccoli.

Combine all the above in a bowl with baby peas and add ¼ of the chicken broth. Combine flour with ½ of the remaining chicken broth and add to mixture. Add cream. You can decide how thick you want the pot pie to be, and just add more broth accordingly. If using parmesan cheese, add it to the mixture. Finally, add peas and herbs. Salt and pepper to taste.

Put <u>hot</u> mixture into serving bowls. Place a square of puff pastry on top, pressing down on the sides. Whisk egg and brush a thin layer over each pastry. Bake at 375°F for 20 minutes or until pastry is puffed and light brown.

Norey's Note:

I heat the chicken mixture first, before I put the puff pastry on.

The pot pie mixture can be refrigerated or frozen. You can also put the mixture over toast!

ENTRÉES

Chinese Orange Shrimp

SERVES: 6

2 pounds fresh shrimp (peeled)
1 teaspoon cornstarch
1 teaspoon baking soda
3–4 tablespoons fresh orange juice
1 tablespoon soy sauce
1 tablespoon rice vinegar
2 tablespoons sesame oil
2 tablespoons peanut oil
1 tablespoon fresh ginger (grated)
4 cloves garlic (chopped)
1 orange rind
2 tablespoons orange peel (grated)
¼ teaspoon crushed red pepper
2 tablespoons fresh cilantro

Norey's Note:

Great flavor! It takes a bit of time to make this dish, but it's well worth it.

You can also substitute beef or boneless chicken instead of shrimp.

TO PREPARE:

Combine cornstarch, baking soda, orange juice, soy sauce, orange rind, and sesame oil. Put shrimp in a bag and fill with enough sauce to cover (reserve extra sauce). Let marinate for several hours.

Heat peanut oil in a wok on high heat, adding the ginger, garlic, grated orange peel, and a dash of crushed red pepper, depending on how spicy you'd like the dish to be. Cook for a few minutes, then add marinated shrimp and stir fry over high heat until crispy. Turn off the heat and add the remaining reserved sauce to the shrimp mixture.

Garnish with chopped fresh cilantro. This is especially good served with cooked white rice, such as jasmine rice.

Judy Cullen's Maryland Crabcakes

SERVES: 6

- 2 large eggs (well beaten)
- ½ cup chopped celery
- 1 cup crushed saltine crackers
- 3 tablespoons mayonnaise
- 1 tablespoon Dijon-style mustard
- 1 teaspoon Old Bay® seasoning
- ¼ teaspoon red pepper flakes
- 2 teaspoons Worchestershire sauce
- 2 tablespoons parsley (finely chopped)
- ½ cup scallions (finely chopped)
- ½ teaspoon salt
- ¼ teaspoon black pepper
- 1 teasoon fresh lemon juice
- 1 teaspoon grated lemon rind
- 1 dash garlic powder
- 1 pound lump crab meat (shell and cartilage removed)
- ½ cup panko breadcrumbs
- 4 tablespoons vegetable oil
- 4 tablespoons butter

TO PREPARE:

Mix panko breadcrumbs in a blender for several seconds to make smaller. In a large mixing bowl, combine eggs, celery, saltines, mayo, mustard, Old Bay Seasoning, red pepper flakes, Worcestershire sauce, parsley, scallions, salt, pepper, lemon juice, lemon rind, and garlic powder. <u>Blend well.</u> Add crab meat, folding it in lightly without breaking it up.

Divide mixture into 10 equal portions and shape into hamburger-like patties. Dredge them lightly in the prepared panko breadcrumbs.

Heat approximately 2 tablespoons of oil and 2 tablespoons butter in a non-stick skillet over medium heat. Sauté the crabcakes for 2–3 minutes on each side or until golden brown. Drain crabcakes on papertowels immediately and serve with fresh lemon and dill sauce — see Norey's Note on right!

Norey's Note:

To make a delicious dill sauce, combine ½ cup mayo, ½ cup sour cream, and ½ teaspoon grated onion.

ENTRÉES

Lemon Chicken with Arugula & Capers

SERVES: 8

3 whole organic boneless chicken breasts

¼ cup vegetable oil

2 lemons (thinly sliced)

4 tablespoons fresh lemon juice

1 cup chicken broth

1 cup half & half

1 cup seasoned panko bread crumbs

(optional) 3 tablespoons capers (chopped)

(optional) 1 avocado (thinly sliced)

arugula

TO PREPARE:

Slice each chicken breast into three pieces and put into a large ziplock bag. Pound until thin. Dip pounded chicken into half & half, then bread crumbs. Set aside until ready to cook.

Heat a 10-inch frying pan with some vegetable oil until hot. Put a few chicken slices into the oiled pan and alternate cooking each side 1 minute, until cooked through and golden brown. Put chicken on a half sheet pan lined with parchment paper for easy reheating.

Sauté sliced lemons on one side over high heat and set aside. When ready to serve, re-heat chicken at 350°F for 10 minutes. Serve on a bed of arugula that has been dressed with a bit of lemon juice and olive oil. Top each piece of chicken with a lemon slice, avocado slice, and a sprinkle of capers.

Norey's Note:

This was one of my most popular dishes at Norey's Restaurant. It is just delicious and you can substitute many different ingredients, such as cooked mushrooms or grilled onions.

It's also a great make-ahead dinner item, as it can be served at room temperature!

Panko bread crumbs are big, so I usually blend them in an electric blender for a minute before using.

ENTRÉES

Norey's Famous Spaghetti and Meat Sauce

SERVES: 8

2 ½ lbs ground beef (85% lean)

(optional) 1 stick butter

½ cup extra virgin olive oil

2 large onions (chopped)

1 6-ounce can tomato paste

3 28-ounce cans crushed tomatoes

7 cloves garlic (or more, thinly sliced)

(optional) 1 cup parmesan cheese

¼ cup dry vermouth or vodka

1 tablespoon sugar

1 ½ tablespoons dried oregano (chopped)

3–4 tablespoons fresh basil (chopped)

1 tablespoon kosher salt & pepper

2 boxes spaghetti

Norey's Note:

Feel free to add more garlic if you like!

You can also substitute vodka for dry vermouth.

TO PREPARE:

Heat olive oil in a large sauté pan over medium-high heat. Add onions and garlic to pan and cook until softened. Add ground beef and cook for 5 minutes. Add tomato paste, crushed tomatoes, sugar, salt, vermouth, and herbs. Cook on low heat for 30 minutes. The sauce should be thick but you can add a little beef broth to thin it to your desired consistency.

Prepare spaghetti *al dente* according to package instructions. Drain in a colander, then return to pot and add 1 stick butter (if desired). Pour sauce on top of pasta. Sprinkle with basil and a good amount of parmesan cheese.

ENTRÉES

Norey's Meatloaf

SERVES: 6

2 ½ pounds meatloaf mix (veal, hamburg, pork)

1 medium onion (chopped)

2 eggs (slightly beaten)

2 packages Knorr's® vegetable soup mix (a must!)

2 tablespoons half & half

3 tablespoons Worcestershire sauce

3 cups breadcrumbs (store-bought is fine)

1 teaspoon oregano

1 tablespoon kosher salt & pepper

(optional) ½ cup ketchup

Norey's Note:

This meatloaf has the texture of a country paté. It makes a terrific sandwich on lightly toasted bread with hot pepper jelly, arugula, and mayo.

TO PREPARE:

Mix all ingredients together in a large bowl. Line a loaf pan with aluminum foil. Put meatloaf mixture into pan and pat down. Spread ketchup on top, and cover pan with aluminum.

Bake at 350°F for 75 minutes. Remove the aluminum and let top brown in the oven for 10 minutes. The meatloaf temperature should read 165°F.

Remove meatloaf from oven and strain any extra juices that may have accumulated in the pan. Let rest for 20 minutes. Cut into 1-inch thick slices, and serve with homemade mashed potatoes and baby peas with butter. Or you can also serve over flat noodles!

P.S. If you make a meatloaf sandwich, I suggest that you sauté a slice or two in a frying pan first. Add mayo to bread, then layer with arugula lettuce and hot pepper jelly.

Oriental Lamb Chops

SERVES: 4

8 thick lamb chops (trimmed of fat)
3 tablespoons Asian sesame oil
1 cup chopped onion
1 tablespoon fresh ginger (peeled & minced)
3 cloves garlic (minced)
3 tablespoons soy sauce
2 tablespoons chili sauce
½ cup orange marmalade
2 tablespoons rice wine vinegar
½ cup cilantro leaves
cooked rice for serving

TO PREPARE:

Heat sesame oil in a heavy sauté pan over medium-high heat. Sauté lamb chops for 2 minutes, flipping halfway through, until medium rare. Drain on paper towels and set aside. (You can also cook lamb chops on a grill and skip the sauté steps above.)

Add onion and garlic to pan and cook until fragrant. Stir in soy sauce, chili sauce, orange marmalade, vinegar, and ginger. Return lamb chops to pan, cover, and cook over low heat for 6–8 minutes while watching the temperature to make sure they don't overcook. Serve over rice, pouring any extra sauce over the chops. Garnish with cilantro.

Poor Man's Potato Pie

SERVES: 6

2 pounds lean ground hamburg or sirloin
1 stick butter (divided)
5 large Idaho potatoes (peeled, cut into chunks)
1 large sweet onion (sliced)
1 pound white mushrooms (sliced)
1 bag frozen petit peas (such as La Sueur®)
3 cloves garlic (chopped)
⅔ cup beef broth
1 cup cream
2 tablespoons fresh basil (chopped)
8 ounces cream cheese (softened)
1 cup cheddar cheese (grated)
1 cup parmesan cheese (grated)
kosher salt & pepper

TO PREPARE:

Bring a large pot of water to boil and add potato chunks, cooking until tender. Drain and return to pot. Using a hand potato masher, mash potatoes with half of the butter, adding cream cheese slowly until soft and fluffy. (It's okay if there are a few lumps, <u>just be sure to avoid using an emulsifier as it can make potatoes sticky!</u>) Salt and pepper to taste, then mix in peas.

Melt remaining butter in a frying pan, and cook sliced onions, mushrooms, and garlic until carmelized. Set aside. Brown the meat in a large skillet over medium heat. Add beef broth, salt, and pepper. Simmer until the beef broth is absorbed, then add basil

<u>To assemble:</u> Spray a 9" x 13" casserole dish with cooking spray. Cover the bottom of the dish with a thin layer of onions and mushrooms. Cover with a layer of half of the mashed potatoes, then all of the ground beef. Make a fourth layer with the remaining onions and mushrooms, and then cover that with the remaining mashed potatoes. Top with the cheddar and parmesan cheeses. Bake at 350°F for 30 minutes.

Norey's Note:

I can't tell you how many times I had this dish as a child, with several variations. We never tired of it!

Serve with a nice clean salad and baked rolls.

Freezes well!

ENTRÉES

ENTRÉES

ENTRÉES

Pork Paillard with Hot Pepper Jelly

SERVES: 6

Norey's Note:

You can use bone-in pork chops instead of tenderloin if you prefer, the process is the same.

This recipe is also delicious with homemade applesauce instead of hot pepper jelly!

1 whole pork tenderloin

1 cup breadcrumbs

1 cup panko breadcrumbs

1 tablespoon oregano

1 tablespoon thyme

2 eggs

2 tablespoons oil

1 teaspoon kosher salt and pepper

1 cup hot pepper jelly

TO PREPARE:

Mix regular and panko breadcrumbs together with oregano, salt, and pepper to season. Cut 2-inch pieces of pork and pound between two pieces of parchment paper until thin. (You can make each piece as big as you want, but pounding it <u>thin</u> is what makes it special.) Stir the eggs in a pan, then dip each piece of pork in the egg then in the breadcrumb mixture to coat.

Heat oil in a frying pan until hot. Add prepared tenderloin pieces in batches and cook on each side until golden brown and crisp. Set cooked pieces aside on a half-sheet pan. Serve each piece with a good amount of hot pepper jelly. Delivious and impressive!

Pork Tenderloin with an Asian Twist

SERVES: 4

1 pork tenderloin

5 cloves garlic (chopped)

¼ cup soy sauce

¼ cup salad oil

4 tablespoons rice vinegar

2 tablespoons brown sugar

½ teaspoon cayenne pepper

1 teaspoon sesame seeds

1 bunch cilantro

Norey's Note:

Be sure the tenderloin is fully cooked, both inside and out.

TO PREPARE:

Leaving cilantro and pork aside, combine all other ingredients in a large jar and shake to mix well. Clean the pork by taking a sharp knife and trimming the sinew off. Put marinade mixture into a large ziplock bag and add cleaned pork. Put in refrigerator for several hours.

Take pork out of refrigerator an hour before putting on the grill, reserving the marinade mixture. Heat the grill and cook pork for 10 minutes (or less) on each side. Let pork rest for 15 minutes before slicing into thin pieces and arranging on a platter. Bring remaining marinade to a boil and cook for 5 minutes. Pour over pork, garnish with fresh cilantro, and serve.

Rosemary Beef Stew the Italian Way

SERVES: 8

2 pounds chuck beef (cut into medium cubes)

3 tablespoons olive oil

2 tablespoons butter

4 cloves garlic (chopped)

1 large onion (chopped)

1 bunch parsley (chopped)

1 cup fresh basil (chopped)

½ teaspoon oregano and thyme

1 28-ounce can peeled tomatoes

½ cup red wine (optional)

2 teaspoons rosemary (fresh is better for this recipe)

parmesan cheese (to garnish)

(optional) ½ cup sliced sun-dried tomatoes

(optional) ⅔ cup green olives

Norey's Note:

Great flavor! If you like sun-dried tomatoes, by all means add some.

TO PREPARE:

Brown the beef on all sides in butter on high heat. Set aside. In same pan, sauté garlic, and onions in olive oil until soft and translucent.

Transfer to a thick dutch oven and add canned tomatoes (squish with your hands before adding), parsley, oregano, thyme, rosemary, and red wine. Cook until sauce just begins to thicken. Add meat and simmer for 1 hour (or longer) until sauce has thickened slightly.

Serve over flat noodles. I like to garnish with fresh chopped basil and a sprinkle of parmesan cheese.

Stuffed Shells My Way

SERVES: 8

1 box large pasta shells
1 tablespoon olive oil
2 bottles Lydia's® tomato basil sauce
1 onion (chopped)
4 cloves garlic (chopped)
1 quart ricotta cheese
1 16-ounch package fresh mozzarella

1 egg
1 teaspoon oregano
1 tablespoon fresh basil
1 tablespoon fresh parsley
1 cup parmesan cheese
kosher salt and cracked pepper

TO PREPARE:

Cook the shells in salted water with a tablespoon of olive oil. Cook about 9 minutes (or until *al dente*) and rinse. Set aside.

Meanwhile, sauté onion and garlic in olive oil on medium heat until translucent. Add Lydia's® sauce, oregano, basil, and parsley. Shred the mozzarella and mix together with the egg and ricotta in a bowl.

To assemble:
Spoon a bit of sauce into the bottom of a 9"x13" pan. Fill the shells with the cheese mixture and arrange in pan with the open side of the shells facing up. Add plenty of sauce on top and sprinkle with parmesan. Bake in the oven at 350°F for 20 minutes or until they are bubbly. Serve with salad.

Norey's Note:

I love this simple dish, and it's an easy go-to for a party with a simple salad and fresh bread.

Other than the oregano, fresh herbs are key to making this dish special. If Lydia's® sauce isn't available at your supermarket, substitute your favorite sauce or make your own! You can also cook hamburg and add that to the shell mixture for a meaty dish.

ENTRÉES

Tyler's Asian Chicken Lettuce Wraps

SERVES: 8

Norey's Note:

Chef Tyler, my second son, bought my restaurant "Norey's" in 2015. Here is one of his popular dishes.

You can use Bibb or butterhead lettuce instead of Boston lettuce if you prefer!

1 head Boston lettuce (washed & dried)
4 boneless chicken breasts (chopped)
1 tablespoon olive oil
1 large bag bean sprouts
1 large onion (chopped)
2 carrots (shredded)
2 cloves garlic (minced)
1 bunch cilantro (lightly chopped)
1 bunch scallions (sliced)

Sauce:
½ cup hoisin sauce
¼ cup Asian sesame oil
(optional) 1 teaspoon red curry paste
4 cloves garlic (minced)
1 ½ tablespoon ginger (chopped)

TO PREPARE:

Chop chicken into very small bites. Heat olive oil, garlic, and onions in a wok (or large frying pan) and sauté for 3 minutes. Add chicken, bean sprouts, and carrots. Cook for a few minutes until chicken is cooked through. Combine all sauce ingredients in a bowl and add to the chicken mixture.

To assemble:
Place 3 pieces of lettuce on a large plate, keeping the leaves intact. Put chicken mixture into a small bowl on the side and garnish with scallions and cilantro.

ENTRÉES

Vegetables

What is better than fresh vegetables, cooked in many different ways? Actually, my favorite are raw vegetables! If you are near a local Farmer's Market, it is always good to buy FRESH veggies. Also, it helps support the local farmers.

I look for good color and hardness/softness depending on what I am buying. I usually buy fruit and vegetables that are NOT totally ripe. I leave them out at room temperature, except for avocados and lettuce, which I refrigerate. I never put tomatoes in the icebox!!

There are so many beautiful colors that can be the "star" of the vegetable dinnerplate! So, when you think of your dinner menu, think about what colors of veggies you want in order to create a pretty and inviting dish for dinner.

Depending on my guests, I sometimes have two or three vegetables with the main dish. And sometimes, I have just vegetables! Some puréed, and some roasted. My favorite way to cook vegetables is to toss them in a bit of good olive oil, rock salt, and pepper, then roast them at 400°F for about 20 minutes.

Learn to be comfortable cooking vegetables in different ways, like roasting, puréeing, blanching, boiling or sautéing in a pan. I prefer my vegetables *al dente*, which means slightly undercooked. An emulsifier is a good tool for puréeing and blending vegetables.

Have FRESH herbs on hand as garnishes for your veggie dishes and soups. I have little pots of fresh herbs in my window during the winter. Fresh herbs are easy to grow outside and most are perennial. They help to bring out the flavor of your vegetables. If you use dried herbs, replace them every year as they don't last forever!! Rock salt is another ingredient that enhances the flavor of different vegetable dishes.

French String Beans with Asian Sauce

SERVES: 6

Norey's Note:

This recipe is really good, and also pairs well with sticky white rice.

1 tablespoon Asian sesame oil

1 tablespoon vegetable oil

1 tablespoon rice vinegar

3 teaspoons soy sauce

1 large clove garlic (chopped fine)

1 tablespoon fresh ginger (chopped)

1 cup sliced almonds

1 large shallot (sliced and fried)

2 lbs French string beans

salt and pepper

pinch of rock salt

2 teaspoons sesame seeds

TO PREPARE:

Put one teaspoon vegetable oil into a frying pan and add almonds and sesame seeds, <u>watching very carefully as they burn easily</u>. When they start to brown, remove from heat, sprinkle with rock salt, and set aside. Add a little more oil to the pan if needed, and fry the shallot slices until crispy.

Put the following into a jar with a lid: sesame oil, vegetable oil, rice vinegar, soy sauce, garlic, ginger, salt, and pepper. Shake the jar until emulsified.

In a covered pot, bring 1 cup of water to a boil. Add string beans and cook for 3 minutes. Remove from pot and <u>immediately</u> run under cold water. They should be *al dente*. Pour mixed sauce over beans and top with crispy shallots, toasted almonds, and sesame seeds. Delicious!

German Golden & Red Beets

SERVES: 6

1 stick butter

3 large golden beets

3 large red beets

2 tablespoons cider vinegar

2 tablespoons sugar

1 teaspoon ground cumin

1 teaspoon kosher salt

TO PREPARE:

I cook the two types of beets separately so the color of red beets doesn't bleed into the golden ones. Rinse beets and cut in half. Arrange on a half sheet pan. Cover with heavy aluminum foil and bake at 375°F for 1 hour or until beet skins peel off easily.

Remove the skin, which should come right off. Cut beets into medium-sized pieces. Add to a frying pan with butter, vinegar, and sugar and cook for 5–8 minutes. Put the beets into a pretty bowl and sprinkle with ground cumin.

Norey's Note:

This "super food" recipe is delicious and has great color! The cumin gives the beets a unique flavor. My mother made these all the time for her dinner parties.

Any beet will work with this recipe. If you are using several different types, keep them separate so their colors don't bleed.

VEGETABLES

Grilled Baby Artichokes with Lemon

SERVES: 6

¼ cup olive oil

2–3 cans artichokes (or frozen)

½ cup fresh lemon juice (fresh is a must!)

1 teaspoon salt

1 teaspoon fresh thyme

Norey's Note:

My son Tyler made these at the restaurant and people loved them!

Two lemons squeezed will get you the amount of fresh lemon juice required for this recipe.

TO PREPARE:

Combine oil, lemon juice, and salt. Marinate artichokes in lemon mixture for at least 1 hour. Arrange artichokes on a grill basket and grill for 2 minutes on each side, or sauté in a cast iron skillet without flipping the artichokes. Garnish with salt and fresh thyme.

Serve as an appetizer or as a side for a meat dish (pairs well with chicken).

Honey Ginger Carrot Purée

SERVES: 6

2 lbs carrots (peeled)

1–2 cups water (as needed to cover carrots)

1 tablespoon orange juice

1 tablespoon pure honey

1 tablespoon finely grated <u>fresh</u> ginger

¾ stick butter

¼ cup apricot preserves

1 teaspoon kosher salt and cracked pepper

TO PREPARE:

Slice carrots in 1-inch pieces and put them into a large pot with just enough water to cover them. Boil about 10 minutes until soft. Put carrots into a blender and purée. Add orange juice, honey, ginger, butter, preserves, salt, and pepper. Pulse a few times to integrate ingredients. Serve as a side dish.

Norey's Note:

Absolutely delicious! A wonderful pairing with almost any meat, and also very colorful!

Rice Casserole

SERVES: 6

5 large egg

3 cups whole milk

1½ cups long grain rice

1 cup parmesan cheese (grated)

Fresh snipped chives

1 teaspoon kosher salt & pepper

Norey's Note:

Make the first part of this dish early in the afternoon as it takes a while for the rice to cool.

Sautéed onions and mushrooms are a nice addition to this tasty meal!

TO PREPARE:

Boil milk in a medium pot and stir in rice. Reduce to a simmer and cook 20 minutes, or until all milk is absorbed. Remove from heat and let rice cool completely.

Separate the yolks from egg whites. Beat egg yolks and add to cooled rice. Whip egg whites until fluffy and add to rice mixture, then add grated cheese. Put mixture into a buttered, medium-size casserole dish and bake at 350°F for 20–25 minutes. *Do not open the oven door!*

Salt and pepper to taste, then garnish with fresh snipped chives.

Tomato Pudding

SERVES: 6

- 5 large vine-ripe tomatoes (seeded & chopped)
- 4 tablespoons butter
- 1 onion (chopped)
- 2 cloves
- 1 ½ tablespoons brown sugar
- pinch of kosher salt
- ¼ cup chili sauce
- 2 tablespoons parsley (chopped)
- 4 slices bread (well toasted, for bread crumbs)
- 1 ½ teaspoons fresh thyme

TO PREPARE:

Melt butter in a frying pan on medium-high heat. Add onions and cloves, and cook for 1–2 minutes. Add the sugar, chili sauce, and tomatoes and stir until well blended.

<u>Remove the cloves.</u> Put the tomato mixture into a shallow buttered dish that can go into the oven. Crumble the toasted bread into crumbs and season with parsley, thyme, and salt. Cover the mixture with the seasoned bread crumbs and bake at 375°F for 20 minutes.

Norey's Note:

This is crazy delicious and men love it with a good steak!

You can also use storebought bread crumbs.

Sautéed Brussels Sprouts & Leeks with Toasted Almonds

SERVES: 6

1 stick butter

24 baby Brussels sprouts (halved)

3 leeks (white part only, sliced)

2 cloves garlic (sliced)

⅔ cup chicken broth (or vegetable)

½ cup heavy cream

pinch nutmeg

kosher salt & pepper

almonds (sliced)

Norey's Note:

Using chicken broth instead of vegetable broth gives this dish a stronger flavor.

TO PREPARE:

Put one teaspoon vegetable oil into a frying pan and add almonds and sesame seeds, watching very carefully as they burn easily. When they start to brown, remove from heat, sprinkle with rock salt, and set aside.

Melt butter in a large frying pan over medium heat. Add Brussels sprouts, leeks, and garlic, and sauté for 10 minutes. Add broth and cover with a lid. Cook until Brussels sprouts are tender (about 15 minutes). Remove lid and add cream. Cook a few more minutes until cream thickens.

Garnish with toasted almonds and serve immediately. This dish is also great with the optional addition of edamame or arugula!

DRESSINGS & SAUCES

Dressings & Sauces

It is important to know what types of dressing is appropriate to what you are making, and the same goes with sauces. Using only the best and freshest ingredients is <u>KEY</u> to the final touch with a sauce. I have a tendency to use too much sauce or dressing, but make sure you drizzle enough so you can taste it. A dressing is the last thing that goes on a dish or salad, and will truly make or break the taste, so put a good effort into preparing your sauce or dressing.

Most dressings last for weeks in the icebox. I put my dressings in a glass jar with a good lid. Let it come to room temperature before using it. Remember that vinegars and olive oil can get old, so know that they don't keep forever after opening.

I've included a number of my favorite dressings and sauces here, but there are so many others that you can find. Don't be shy in asking a friend about what ingredients he or she used for a lunch or dinner salad. We all love to share our "secrets" so others can enjoy.

1000 Island Dressing

1 cup Hellmann's® mayonnaise
1 tablespoon cider or white vinegar
1 cup sour cream
½ cup chili sauce
½ cup sweet relish (<u>drained well</u>)
½ cup chives (fresh, chopped)
½ cucumber (peeled, chopped fine)

TO PREPARE:

Combine all ingredients in a glass jar. Close the lid tightly and shake until well mixed. This dressing also freezes well, and will last up to two weeks in an icebox.

Norey's Note: I love this dressing on a Mexican salad or a roast beef sandwich.

Caesar Salad Dressing

2 large garlic cloves (finely chopped)
1 egg yolk
1 teaspoon Dijon mustard
1 tablespoon Worchestershire sauce
¼ cup olive oil
¼ cup vegetable oil
1 teaspoon pesto sauce
½ cup parmesan cheese (grated)
2 tablespoons white wine vinegar

TO PREPARE:

Combine all ingredients in a glass jar. Close the lid tightly and shake until well mixed. Drizzle over my Elegant Caesar Salad (pg. 75).

Norey's Note: If you like anchovies, feel free to add one minced anchovy to this recipe!

David's Sesame Ginger Dressing

2 tablespoons light brown sugar
3 tablespoons soy sauce
3 tablespoons sesame oil
2 tablespoons olive oil
2 tablespoons rice vinegar
2 tablespoons lemon juice
½ teaspoon tumeric
1 tablespoon garlic (mashed)
1 tablespoon fresh ginger (mashed)
1 teaspoon thyme (fresh if possible)
salt & pepper

TO PREPARE:

Mix all ingredients in a lidded jar. This will store in the icebox for a long time. Delicious over salad or hot broccoli/cauliflower. I have also added salted toasted almonds (pg. 143).

Norey's Note: This recipe comes from my son, David. It's a very unusual dressing which can be used in many ways, such as a dip or even on a pasta! It's also good on boneless grilled chicken.

Honey Lemon Vinaigrette

2 garlic cloves (halved)
¼ cup olive oil
¼ cup regular salad oil
1 large lemon (zested)
3 tablespoons fresh lemon juice
1 teaspoon Dijon mustard
2 tablespoons apple cider vinegar
2 tablespoons pure raw honey
1 teaspoon kosher salt and pepper

TO PREPARE:

Combine all ingredients in a glass jar. Close the lid tightly and shake until well mixed. Serve with any salad greens. It can easily be doubled and refrigerated—it will last several months in the icebox. Try adding sliced avocado, toasted almonds, and golden raisins to the dressing for some extra flavor. It's also delicious on oysters or for sautéing chicken!

Nina's Roquefort & Anchovy Dressing

2 cups Hellman's® mayonnaise
2 garlic cloves (minced)
⅓ cup scallions (chopped)
2 tablespoons anchovy paste
1 cup sour cream

½ cup white wine vinegar
2 tablespoons lemon juice
½ pound Roquefort cheese
½ cup parsley (chopped)
1 teaspoon kosher salt and pepper

TO PREPARE:

Mix all ingredients together in a jar with a lid. This is delicious with tomato aspic or any variety of lettuce, as well as over shrimp or scallops.

Norey's Note: My sister, Nina Dotterer, is a fantastic cook! This dressing has a real "bite" to it.

Spinach Salad Dressing
(from the Black Pearl)

1 pound bacon (crispy, crumbled)
1 cup tarragon wine vinegar
3 cups salad oil
2 egg yolks
2 teaspoons Dijon mustard (heaping)

½ teaspoon seasoned salt (to taste)
1 teaspoon kosher salt (to taste)
1 teaspoon cracked pepper (to taste)
1 teaspoon sugar
2 or 3 ounces bleu cheese (crumbled)

TO PREPARE:

Combine all ingredients in an electric blender and blend until creamy. Warm dressing in a frying pan just before serving. Serve with baby white mushrooms, crumbled bacon, thinly sliced red onions, and baby spinach. Dressing will keep in the icebox for up to one month.

Norey's Note: Try adding dried cranberries or sliced fresh apples!

Sweet Balsamic Dressing

1 tablespoon olive oil
1 cup salad oil
½ cup good quality balsamic vinegar
1 tablespoon Dijon mustard
½ cup sugar (or more)
½ teaspoon thyme
½ teaspoon kosher salt & pepper

TO PREPARE:

Mix all ingredients together in a large bowl and whisk, or put into a medium-sized glass jar and shake vigorously. The salad dressing will become thick. Serve over any salad or use as a dipping sauce for cheddar cheese cubes, chicken, pork, etc. It is very versatile and will last for weeks in your icebox!

Norey's Note: This was the most popular salad dressing at my restaurant; so much so that we hardly made anything else! I finally decided to bottle it as there were so many requests.

Asian Sweet Sauce

1 cup low sodium soy sauce
½ cup sherry
4 garlic cloves (minced)
1 tablespoon fresh ginger (minced)
2 tablespoons sesame peanut oil
1 cup brown sugar

TO PREPARE:

In a medium sauce pan, combine all ingredients and cook until it comes to a boil. Turn off the heat and let sit until cool. Pour into a plastic container and reheat to serve with any Asian or Thai food. It will last a month in the icebox.

Norey's Note: A very versatile sauce that can be used with any Asian recipe.

A Different Pesto

1 stick butter (softened)
½ cup olive oil (or more)
5 cloves garlic
½ cup parmesan romano cheese

8 ounces cream cheese (softened)
½ cup pignoli nuts (chopped)
4 cups fresh basil

TO PREPARE:

Blend nuts in food processor with olive oil. Slowly add the rest of the ingredients and blend until sauce has a creamy consistancy. Use with any pasta dish or on bruschetta with roasted plum tomatoes and goat cheese. This sauce will last several weeks in a well-sealed container in the icebox. It also freezes well—you can pour the sauce into ice trays and reheat the frozen cubes as needed!

Norey's Note: I like this pesto, which is a bit different with the addition of cream cheese.

Bourbon Sauce

1 stick butter
1 cup heavy cream
2 cups sugar

1 tablespoon pure vanilla
¼ cup bourbon
(optional) ½ teaspoon kosher salt

TO PREPARE:

Melt butter in a small saucepan. Add sugar and stir for 10 minutes or until it turns golden brown. Slowly add the heavy cream and continue cooking for 5 minutes until it thickens slightly. Turn off the heat and add in the bourbon and vanilla. If the sauce gets crumbly after adding the cream, strain it and discard the hard crumbles.

This sauce will last for weeks in the icebox. When ready to serve, warm it up in the microwave and drizzle over your favorite dessert!

Lime Sauce

1 cup Hellmann's® mayonnaise
2 teaspoons lime zest
⅓ cup fresh or bottled lime juice (or more)
1 cup sour cream
1 teaspoon Dijon mustard

½ teaspoon white horseradish (optional)
1 cup cilantro (chopped)
½ teaspoon kosher salt
½ teaspoon cracked pepper

TO PREPARE:

Grate the lime until you have 2 teaspoons of zest. Mix all ingredients together in a bowl and refrigerate for several hours. Serve over your favorite fish or lobster dishes. This sauce will last 4–5 days in the icebox.

Norey's Note: This sauce can also serve as a refreshing dip to crudités.

Norey's Beurre Blanc Sauce

6 shallots (finely chopped)
¾ cup white wine vinegar
3 sticks unsalted butter (melted)

TO PREPARE:

Simmer shallots in vinegar over medium-high heat for 10 minutes. Strain out the shallots, leaving the vinegar in the pan. Add the melted butter to the vinegar and continue to cook until smooth — it should get thick. Keep warm over a double boiler until ready to serve. <u>Do not reheat</u>, it does not keep well!

Norey's Note: A delicious and versatile sauce which can be used on fish, chicken, steak, and vegetables such as asparagus and broccoli.

Peanut Sauce (My Way!)

1 tablespoon honey
½ cup cilantro (chopped)
½ teaspoon fresh ginger (grated)
2 tablespoons Asian sesame oil
¾ can coconut milk
1 cup peanut butter
1 ½ tablespoon rice vinegar
(optional) lime juice

TO PREPARE:

Blend all ingredients in a food processor. This versatile sauce is especially delicious on chicken, pasta, or as a salad dressing.

Norey's Note: I use peanut sauce on so many of my recipes! Be sure your guests do not have peanut allergies.

Homemade Bread Crumbs

2 loaves bread (several days old)
2 cups parmesan cheese
1 tablespoon oregano, basil, and parsley (mixed)
1 tablespoon salt & pepper

TO PREPARE:

Put all ingredients into a food processor and pulse until the bread is fine. Refrigerate and store in a ziplock bag. Use in any recipe that calls for bread crumbs.

Norey's Note: Whole wheat or white bread works best. Delicious!

Roasted Pecans

2 cups pecans (or almonds, or walnuts)
1 or 2 egg whites
2 tablespoons sugar
1 teaspoon kosher salt
½ teaspoon cayenne pepper

TO PREPARE:

Toss ingredients with pecans. Spread evenly on a sheet pan and bake at 400°F for about 8 minutes. <u>Watch carefully</u> as they can burn easily! Turn pecans with a spatula several times while baking to make sure both sides get crisp. When cool, break into pieces and sprinkle on your salad, dessert, or any fruit. Store in a tin can.

Salted Toasted Almonds

1 teaspoon olive oil
2 cups sliced almonds (preferably skin off)
1 teaspoon kosher sea salt

TO PREPARE:

Heat a large frying pan on medium heat. Add olive oil and almonds. *Stir constantly as they burn <u>very easily</u>! Don't leave the stove at all.* When the almonds start to turn light brown, they are done. Sprinkle the toasted almonds with sea salt. Store in a glass jar or ziplock bag.

Norey's Note: You can't make enough of this superfood! The minute I make these, I hide them as my family will devour them! They are so delicious and are wonderful on salads in particular.

BREAD PUDDING

Bread Pudding

I think I could write an entire cookbook just on different bread puddings! My mother made bread pudding all the time, especially in the winter. She made every kind imaginable. I didn't really like bread pudding as a child, but now they are one of my absolute favorite dishes, and the sweet varieties were the most popular of all my desserts at Norey's.

So, what's the secret to bread pudding? Obviously, the bread! I only use three types of bread for my "sweet" puddings: croissants, cinnamon raisin bread, and Portuguese sweet bread. For my savory puddings, I use ciabatta bread, or any leftover rolls or croissants (my favorite is croissants!). It is a must that the pudding be served warm! You can microwave it if it gets too cool.

My bread puddings require a water bath, which is simply putting the baking dish with all ingredients into a larger pan half-filled with water — the water should reach about ¼ of the way up the side of the dish (see below). Be careful when removing the pudding dish from the hot water bath!

I like bread puddings as you can make them the day before serving, and they can last for several days in the icebox. They freeze well as long as you wrap them carefully! You can also cut bread pudding with cookie cutters for different occasions, although you'll waste some of it.

Bread pudding is a wonderful "comfort food" in the winter, but I also make it in the summer with fresh summer fruits like peaches, blueberries, and blackberries. It must be served warm over heavy cream on the bottom of the plate, or topped with fresh whipped cream. Add a sprig of fresh mint as a garnish.

Bread pudding baking dish inside a larger water bath pan.

Artichoke & Baby Broccoli with Goat & Manchego Cheese

SERVES: 8

8 or 9 croissants (cut into pieces)

1 tablespoon olive oil

2 packages frozen artichoke hearts

1 bunch broccoli (cut into small florets)

2 large cloves garlic (minced)

1 large onion (chopped)

1 bunch parsley (chopped)

1 8-ounce package goat cheese

1 pound manchego cheese (sliced thin)

1 teaspoon fresh thyme

1 ½ quarts whipping cream

5 eggs

1 teaspoon kosher salt & cracked pepper (or more)

TO PREPARE:

Cook broccoli in water with salt until tender. Sauté onion, garlic, and artichokes in olive oil until golden. Cut bread and croissants into bite-size pieces and put half into a greased 10" x 15" glass baking dish. Layer broccoli, artichoke mixture, manchego, and goat cheese over bread pieces, then top with the remaining bread.

Mix eggs and whipping cream in a bowl, and pour over the prepared bread. Season with salt and pepper, then bake at 350°F for 75 minutes.

Mushroom, Onion & Cheese Bread Pudding

SERVES: 8

- 10 large croissants
- 1 stick butter (melted)
- 2 pounds white button mushrooms (sliced)
- 2 onions (thinly sliced)
- 5 large eggs
- 1 cup gruyere cheese (grated)
- 2 cups cheddar cheese (grated)
- 1 ½ quarts cream
- ½ teaspoon nutmeg
- 1 bunch fresh basil (chopped)
- 1 cup fresh parsley (chopped)
- 1 ½ teaspoons kosher salt and pepper

TO PREPARE:

Grease a 10" x 15" pan. Cut croissants into cubes and put half into pan. Melt butter in a large saucepan and sauté onions, garlic, and mushrooms until caramelized. Add chopped parsley and pour half of mixture over croissant cubes. Mix the cheeses together and add half, then top with the remaining half of croissant cubes and remaining half of mushroom mixture.

Mix eggs, cream, nutmeg, chopped basil, salt, and pepper together in a mix master. Pour over croissants and top with remaining cheese. Put pudding pan into a larger pan filled with enough water to reach ¼ of the way up the side of the pudding pan. Bake at 350°F for 75 minutes in a water bath. Remove the pudding pan carefully from the hot water bath and serve.

Norey's Note:

This savory bread pudding is a delicious accompaniment to any meat dish or as a main course with a side salad.

I like to serve them at luncheons. This is also a great dish for vegetarians!

If you're not a fan of gruyere or cheddar, you can really choose whatever cheese you like.

Roasted Corn, Onion & Cheddar Bread Pudding

SERVES: 10

10 croissants

1 stick butter (melted)

6 ears of fresh corn (cut off the cob)

1 28-ounce can of creamed corn

2 medium onions (chopped)

5 eggs

1 ½ quarts cream

3 cups sharp cheddar cheese

2 tablespoons fresh basil (chopped)

1 or 2 teaspoons kosher salt and pepper

TO PREPARE:

Pre-heat oven to 350°F. Spray a 10" x 15" pan with cooking spray. Cut croissants into bite-size cubes and put half into pan.

Sauté onions in butter until soft. Add fresh corn and continue sautéing for several minutes until corn is <u>slightly</u> caramelized. Mix in the creamed corn. Pour the corn mixture on croissants and cover with ⅔ of the cheddar cheese. Top with remaining croissant pieces.

Mix cream, eggs, basil, salt, and pepper together in a mix master and pour over bread mixture. Top with remaining cheese and bake at 350°F for 75 minutes. Let rest for at least 30 minutes before cutting into squares. Sprinkle with any fresh herbs before serving.

Norey's Note:

If you want to spice things up, slice up a jalapeño pepper and sauté it with the onions!

BREAD PUDDING

SAVORY

Chocolate Raisin Bread Pudding

SERVES: 10

2 loaves cinnamon raisin bread (I use Pepperidge Farm®)

5 large eggs

3 cups sugar

1 8-ounce bag chocolate chips, good quality

1 cup golden raisins

1 cup unsweetened cocoa powder

1 ½ quarts cream

1 tablespoon pure vanilla extract

TO PREPARE:

Spray a 10" x 15" glass baking pan with cooking spray. Cut bread into medium-sized cubes and put half into pan. Add chocolate chips and raisins, then top with remaining bread.

Mix cream and 3 cups sugar together in a mix master and add eggs one at a time. Add cocoa and vanilla, and pour over bread (make sure it is mixed well). Sprinkle with remaining sugar.

Put baking pan into a water bath, adding water about a quarter of the way up the pan's edge. Bake at 350°F for 75 minutes, then let sit for an hour to cool. Cut into squares and put on a small plate. Serve warm, topped with vanilla ice cream or fresh whipped cream and perhaps a drizzle of chocolate sauce.

Norey's Note:

I made this all the time for my restaurant. People just love it!

This reheats easily in the microwave. It is a must that this dish be served warm!

Coconut Bread Pudding

SERVES: 8–10

10 croissants

1 can cream of coconut milk

1 quart cream

3 cups sugar (separated)

2 tablespoon pure vanilla

5 eggs

2 cups coconut

TO PREPARE:

Spray or butter a 10" x 15" pan to grease. Cut croissants into bite-size pieces and put half into the pan. Spread toasted coconut over the bread, then add remaining half of croissants.

Set 3 tablespoons of sugar aside. Mix the cream, coconut milk, remaining sugar, eggs, and vanilla together by hand. Pour over bread, and sprinkle the 3 tablespoons of sugar on top of pudding. Put the bread pudding into a water bath, and bake at 350°F for 80 minutes.

Serve with fresh whipped cream. Delicious!

Fresh Blueberry Bread Pudding

SERVES: 10

10 large croissants

2 boxes fresh or wild blueberries

5 eggs

1 ½ quarts medium cream

2 teaspoons pure vanilla extract

1 teaspoon cinnamon

3 cups sugar (separated)

TO PREPARE:

Spray a 10" x 15" pan with cooking spray. Cut croissants into bite-size pieces and put half into the pan. Layer blueberries on top, then cover with remaining croissant pieces. Sprinkle with ⅛ cup sugar.

Mix cream, eggs, cinnamon, 3 cups of sugar, and vanilla together in a mix master and pour over croissants. Sprinkle remaining sugar on top of the bread. Bake in water bath at 350°F for 75 minutes. Serve warm with vanilla ice cream and whipped cream. Garnish with a sprig of fresh mint.

BREAD PUDDING

SWEET

Fresh Peach Bread Pudding

SERVES: 10

10 large croissants

6–7 fresh ripe peaches (peeled & sliced)

3 ⅛ cups sugar (separated)

5 eggs

1 ½ quarts medium cream

2 teaspoons pure vanilla extract

2 tablespoons peach liquor

TO PREPARE:

Spray a 10" x 15" pan with cooking spray. Cut croissants into bite-size pieces and put half into the pan. Layer peaches on top, then cover with remaining croissant pieces.

Mix eggs, cream, 3 cups sugar, vanilla, and peach schnapps together in a mix master and pour over croissants. Drizzle peach liquor overtop if desired. Sprinkle remaining sugar on top of the bread. Put pudding pan into water bath and bake at 350°F for 75 mintues. Serve warm with vanilla ice cream or whipped cream. Garnish with a sprig of fresh mint.

Norey's Note:

This receipe is my favorite!

It is a <u>must</u> that you use fresh peaches. The peaches are key to this wonderful pudding, so feel free to use more than directed.

Peanut Butter & Jelly Bread Pudding

SERVES: 8–10

10 croissants

5 eggs

2 cups peanut butter (melted)

2 cups strawberry preserves (melted)

1 ½ quarts medium cream

3 ⅛ cups sugar

2 tablespoons vanilla

TO PREPARE:

Spray a 10" x 15" glass pan with cooking spray. Cut croissants into cubes and put half into the pan. Melt peanut butter in the microwave. Spread over bread, then do the same with strawberry preserves over peanut butter. Add remaining croissant cubes on top. Mix 3 cups sugar, eggs, vanilla, and cream together and pour overtop.

Sprinkle with the remaining sugar and put the pudding pan into a water bath. Cook at 350°F for 75 minutes. Serve warm, topped with ice cream or fresh whipped cream. (I prefer whipped cream!)

Norey's Note:

Who doesn't like a good old PB&J? I actually came up with this recipe by mistake, and it ended up being a hit at my restaurant!

Pineapple Almond Bread Pudding

SERVES: 10

1 fresh ripe pineapple (peeled)
1 14-ounce can crushed pineapple
5 large eggs
1 cup toasted almonds (optional)
2 large loaves Portuguese sweet bread
1 ½ quarts cream
3 cups sugar
1 tablespoon pure vanilla extract
1 teaspoon salt
½ cup sugar for sprinkling

Norey's Note:

This is a great recipe for an Easter lunch or dinner, and is especially great if you're having a buffet!

TO PREPARE:

Spray a 10" x 15" glass pan with cooking spray. Cut bread into small pieces; layer half in the pan. Drain the crushed pineapple (reserving the juice). Cut the fresh pineapple into small pieces and mix with crushed pineapple, then spread over the bread. Layer the remaining bread on top.

With a large whisk, mix cream, eggs, sugar, vanilla, and reserved pineapple juice together. Pour over prepared bread mixture. Sprinkle with sugar.

Put pan into a water bath and cook at 350°F for 75 minutes. Serve warm with whipped cream or top with toasted almonds. This will last several days and is both freezable and microwaveable.

Vanilla Bourbon Bread Pudding

SERVES: 8

10 croissants

5 large eggs

1 ½ quarts medium cream

1 tablespoon pure vanilla extract

3 cups sugar

1 teaspoon kosher salt

½ cup good quality bourbon
    (or more, I like Maker's Mark®)

caramel sauce

sugar for sprinkling

TO PREPARE:

Spray a 10" x 15" pan with cooking spray. Cut croissants into bite-size pieces and arrange in the pan until they fill it to the top.

Mix cream, sugar, eggs, vanilla, bourbon, and salt together in a mix master and pour over the bread. Sprinkle extra sugar all over the top. Put the pan in a water bath and bake at 350°F for 75 minutes. It should be golden-brown.

Cut into squares and serve warm with vanilla ice cream, and drizzle with caramel sauce.

This lasts for 4 or 5 days. make sure you heat servings for a minute in the microwave before serving. It needs to be eaten warm!

Norey's Note:

This bread pudding is especially good in the fall and winter. A caramel sauce goes nicely with it, plus fresh whipped cream.

CAKES

Cakes

I use parchment paper liner when baking cakes, and spray the liner with cooking spray before pouring batter into pans. Always allow cream cheese, butter, eggs, and sour cream to come to room remperature so that the ingredients are soft enough to mix well.

<u>Don't</u> use substitutes for cakes — especially not margerine or low-fat cream cheese! It is also important to use <u>pure</u> vanilla.

Your finger is a good test to see if a cake is done. Just gently press a finger into the center of the cake. If the cake springs back up, it's done! Otherwise, a toothpick inserted into the center of the cake will come out clean when the cake is fully baked.

When it comes to frosting, <u>make sure cakes are completely cooled before you start to frost!</u> When frosting a cake, one option is to first put a thin layer of frosting all over the cake. Refrigerate for 30 minutes, then add remaining frosting to the first coat. This will give it a smooth finish. I like to use a "Lazy Susan" to easily rotate cakes while frosting.

To keep your cakes fresh, invest in a cake storage container (usually plastic), as it will keep cake fresh and very moist for several days. Keep cakes at room temperature in a cake tin, or put in the icebox after two days to keep it fresh. You can freeze unfrosted cake wrapped very tightly in Saran® wrap and aluminum foil. You can also freeze frosting in a plastic container, just be sure to label the date and type of frosting on the container.

Best Lemon Cream Cheese Pound Cake

SERVES: 10

2 sticks butter
3 cups sugar
zest from 2 lemons
juice from 2 lemons
6 large eggs
1 8-ounce package cream cheese (softened)
1 tablespoon pure vanilla extract
3 cups flour
1 teaspoon baking soda
1 teaspoon baking powder
1 teaspoon kosher salt

Glaze:
1 ¼ cup powdered sugar
2 tablespoons lemon juice

TO PREPARE:

Combine butter, cream cheese, and sugar in a mix master and add eggs one at a time. Make sure to scrape down the sides of the bowl after each addition. Add the lemon zest and 2 tablespoons (or more) lemon juice to the mixture.

Add salt, baking powder, baking soda, and flour. Spray a large bundt pan with cooking spray and pour batter into pan. Bake at 350°F for 45–50 minutes. Let the cake cool completely. Run a knife along the edge of the pan to loosen cake before removing.

Glaze: Mix powdered sugar and remaining lemon juice until smooth. Pour over piping hot cake immediately after removing from oven.

Norey's Note:

An old-fashioned and delicious cake. Serve with mixed berries and fresh whipped cream.

CAKES

Chocolate Raisin Sticky Toffee Pudding Cake

SERVES: 8

1 stick butter (softened)
½ cup brown sugar
3 medium eggs
1 teaspoon pure vanilla
½ teaspoon salt
1 cup flour (heaping)
1 pound fresh dates (pitted, chopped)
1 cup water
1 teaspoon baking soda
8 ounces chocolate chips, melted)
1 cup golden raisins

Norey's Note:

This is absolutely delicious with a dollop of fresh whipped cream.

TO PREPARE:

Put butter and brown sugar into a mix master for a few minutes, then add eggs one at a time. Add salt and flour to mixture. Cook dates in water for 5 minutes and add baking soda (it should bubble up). Add date mixture to the mixer.

Melt chocolate in a microwave or small pan on the stove. Add chocolate and golden raisins to mixer. Butter a 9 ½-inch pie pan and pour in mixture. Bake at 350°F for 30 minutes. When done, prick holes in cake and pour my Bourbon Sauce (pg. 140) on this cake — a must!

Dense Dark Chocolate Mini Cupcakes

SERVES: 12

3 sticks butter (softened)

3 cups sugar

5 extra large eggs (room temperature)

1 cup buttermilk (room temperature)

3 cups flour

1 tablespoon pure vanilla extract

1 tablespoon instant coffee

1 cup dark cocoa powder

1 teaspoon baking powder

1 teaspoon baking soda

1 teaspoon salt

1 mini cupcake pan

Norey's Note:

This is one of my most popular cakes. It is so versatile!

TO PREPARE:

Cream butter and sugar together in a food processor, then add eggs one at a time. Add buttermilk and vanilla. Sift together baking powder, baking soda, cocoa, instant coffee, and flour, then add to mixture.

Spray the cupcake pan with cooking spray or vegetable oil. Divide batter evenly. Bake at 350°F for 18–20 minutes. Be sure not to over cook. Let cool completely before topping with your choice of frosting.

These mini one-bite cakes are so great at the end of a party! This recipe can also be made as a cake — instead of a cupcake pan, use 3 cake pans sprayed with vegetable oil.

Ginger Cheesecake

SERVES: 8

2 tablespoons crystallized ginger (finely chopped)

1 tablespoon grated fresh ginger

2 teaspoons powdered ginger

5 eggs (room temperature)

5 8-ounce packages of cream cheese (softened)

3 cups sugar

1 tablespoon pure vanilla

Crust:

1 stick butter (melted)

½ cup sugar

2 packages ginger snap cookies

Norey's Note:

I love fresh ginger! This recipe is very popular, incorporating the ginger snap crust, crystallized ginger, and of course, fresh ginger, which is so good for you.

TO PREPARE:

Crust: Combine ginger snaps and ½ cup sugar in a food processor and pulse until snaps are finely ground. Melt butter and mix into the crumbled snaps. Press mixture into a 9-inch springform pan.

Cake mixture: Preheat oven to 350°F. Combine cream cheese and sugar in a mix master on medium speed until smooth. Add eggs one at a time.

Peel and grate the fresh ginger, and add it to the cream cheese mixture. Add vanilla, crystallized ginger, and powdered ginger. Pour into a springform pan. Put cheesecake in a water bath and bake at 350°F for 75 minutes. Let it sit in the oven for 30 minutes. Remove from oven, cover with Saran® wrap, and put into the icebox for 24 hours. Remove from pan and garnish with fresh mint before serving.

CAKES

Mom's Honeycrisp Apple Cake with Walnuts

SERVES: 12

- 3 honeycrisp apples (peeled & chopped)
- 1½ cups vegetable oil
- 3 cups sugar
- ¼ cup fresh orange juice
- 5 eggs (room temperature)
- ½ cup walnuts (chopped)
- 3 cups flour
- 2 teaspoons pure vanilla extract
- 1 teaspoon cinnamon
- 1 teaspoon baking powder
- 1 teaspoon baking soda
- 1 teaspoon kosher salt

TO PREPARE:

Preheat oven to 350°F. Spray a 10-inch tube pan. Combine sugar and oil in a mix master and add eggs one at a time. Add orange juice and vanilla.

Add flour, baking powder, baking soda, and salt to liquid mixture. Peel apples and chop into small pieces. Chop nuts and add to mixture along with chopped apples. Bake at 350°F for 50 minutes. Stick a knife or toothpick in to check that it is done before removing from the oven.

Cream cheese frosting is great with this cake, but you can also just sprinkle powdered sugar on top if you don't want it to be too sweet! Or combine 2 cups powdered sugar with ¼ cup half-and-half and drizzle over cake!

Norey's Note:

This is a dense cake with a great taste; not too sweet. It is perfect for afternoon tea or a fall luncheon. A very flavorful cake.

Feel free to substitute pecans or cashews for the walnuts.

Peanut Butter Cream Cheese Cake

SERVES: 8

2 cups sugar
4 eggs (room temperature)
1 ½ cups peanut butter
5 8-ounce packages cream cheese (room temp)
1 cup sour cream
1 tablespoon pure vanilla

Crust:
½ cup sugar
2 cups golden graham cracker crumbs
1 stick butter (melted)
1 teaspoon cinnamon

Norey's Note:

This cake is a peanut butter and cream cheese lover's dream.

It's extra delicious with melted chocolate drizzled on top!

TO PREPARE:

Crust: Pre-heat oven to 350°F. Mix 3 tablespoons sugar, graham cracker crumbs, melted butter, and cinnamon together, and press into a 10-inch springform pan.

Cake mixture: In a mix master, combine cream cheese, remaining sugar, peanut butter, and sour cream. Add eggs one at a time, then add vanilla. Pour mixture into graham cracker crust.

Bake in a water bath for 75 minutes. Turn oven off and keep cake in oven with door open for 30 minutes. Cover with Saran® wrap and refrigerate for several hours or overnight. Run a sharp knife around the springform pan to release the cake.

CAKES

CAKES

Sour Cream Butter Cake

SERVES: 12

3 sticks butter (room temp)

3 cups sugar

5 eggs

1 ½ cups sour cream

1 tablespoon pure vanilla

3 cups flour (sifted)

1 teaspoon baking soda

1 teaspoon baking powder

1 teaspoon salt

Frosting:

2 sticks butter (softened)

¼ cup half & half (warm)

1 2-pound bag confectioner's sugar

1 tablespoon pure vanilla

TO PREPARE:

Cake: Preheat oven to 350°F. In a mix master, cream together butter and sugar for about 3 minutes. Add eggs one at a time. Mix in sour cream, salt, baking soda, baking powder, and vanilla. Slowly add in the flour until well-blended.

Line three 9" cake pans with parchment paper and coat the lining with either butter or cooking spray. Divide the mixture into the prepared pans. Bake for 20 minutes or until the cake bounces back when you gently press your finger into it. Let the cake cool completely (overnight is best) before frosting.

Frosting: Mix all frosting ingredients in a mix master until smooth. If frosting is too thick, add more cream until easily spreadable.

Norey's Note:

I dream about this cake!

Ultimate Carrot Cake

SERVES: 10–12

1 ½ cup vegetable oil (do not use olive oil!)
3 cups sugar
5 eggs
1 ripe banana
3 cups carrots (peeled & grated)
1 cup golden raisins
(optional) ½ cup crushed pineapple (drained well)
(optional) 1 cup pecans (chopped)
3 cups flour
1 tablespoon pure vanilla extract
1 teaspoon baking soda
1 teaspoon kosher salt

Frosting:
1 ½ stick butter (softened)
8 ounces cream cheese (softened)
1 tablespoon pure vanilla
1 2-pound bag of powdered sugar (or more)
3 tablespoons cream (for thinning if needed)

TO PREPARE:

Cake: Put parchment paper into three 9-inch cake pans and spray with cooking spray. In a mix master, combine sugar and oil, then add eggs one at a time. Add baking soda, salt, and vanilla to the mixture.

Add grated carrots, bananas, chopped pecans, oatmeal, raisins, and crushed pineapple. Gradually add flour. Pour into prepared cake pans, and bake at 350°F for 20 minutes. Check for done-ness by pushing your finger on top — it should quickly spring back up.

Frosting: Thoroughly mix all frosting ingredients in a mix master. If frosting is too thick, add cream. Frost between each layer and over the entire cake.

Norey's Note:

I have made this cake so many times in the past 15 years. It was the most asked-for dessert at my restaurant!

CAKES

COOKIES

Cookies

Nothing is better than a homemade cookie!!! I rarely buy store-bought cookies unless it's an emergency. I especially enjoy the many varieties of shortbread, including oat, ginger, apricot, raisin, and honey chocolate shortbreads. Then there is the forever famous chocolate chip cookie with its many varieties.

The process of baking cookies is important. I like to use a thicker cookie sheet for my cookies. Most cookie sheets don't need to be greased unless you are making meringue. I always try to watch my cookies because they can easily burn. Let the baked cookies cool for a few minutes before taking a spatula to remove them.

There are different methods of cooking for chewy and crisp cookies. For chewy cookies with soft centers, place spoonfuls of dough on the cookie sheet and put the whole thing into the icebox for 15–20 minutes. Then put the pan into a preheated 350°F oven and cook in accordance with the recipe. For chewy brownies, cook them in a 325°F oven and when finished, the edges will look more done than the center. Do not overbake!

For crisp cookies, put the dough on the cookie sheet and pat the center down. Let the dough cook thoroughly at the temperature provided in the recipe. Make sure you completely cool the cookies before you store them. Cookies have a good shelf life… at least three weeks or longer as long as they are in an airtight container.

You can also freeze cookie dough. Wrap it carefully in parchment paper and then put the dough in a ziplock bag. If not properly wrapped, the cold air will get into the cookie dough and ruin it. Write a date on the bag, and it normally lasts several months. Around Christmas, I like to make a cookie dough in advance and freeze it since I make so many cookies for presents. It's convenient to just pull out the dough from the freezer and get going on the cookies.

I don't think you can give a nicer present than a box of homemade cookies!! Get creative with pretty wrapping paper or possibly a special decorated box. I usually throw in some kind of chocolate fudge or candy, and top the gift with a candy cane or two. A truly great gift!!

One last word of advice: be careful when packing cookies to mail. Make sure they are laying flat in ziplock bags. I always put cookie boxes into another larger box and surround the inner box with crushed paper to protect them.

Almond Apricot Shortbread

Norey's Note:

Just another delicious shortbread recipe in another shape! A great way to use apricots and almonds.

1 cup butter (cut into pieces)

1 cup powdered sugar

2 egg yolks

1 egg

zest of 2 lemons

2 cups flour

1 tablespoon pure vanilla

1 teaspoon salt

1 cup apricot preserves

2 cups almonds

1 tablespoon milk

1 tablespoon sugar

TO PREPARE:

Using a food processor, process almonds until they are finely ground and set aside. Put butter, sugar, lemon zest, flour, and egg yolks into processor and process until mixed well. Add chopped almonds and mix until evenly distributed.

Put dough on a piece of parchment paper and refrigerate for an hour. Once chilled, roll out the dough and cut into two pieces. Place one piece of dough into a 9" x 13" pan. Spread a good amount of apricot preserves on top of dough and add the remaining dough on top of preserves. Beat the remaining egg with sugar and milk then brush the mixture over the pastry with a pastry brush. Bake for about 10 minutes at 400°F. Reduce heat to 350°F and bake for 30 more minutes until done. Cool and cut into rectangles, then dust with powdered sugar.

COOKIES

Butter Roll Cookies with Apricot Jam

2 sticks butter
⅔ cup confectioner's sugar
½ teaspoon kosher salt
1 teaspoon pure vanilla syrup

2 ½ cups flour
1 cup apricot jam
1 egg

TO PREPARE:

Mix all ingredients except jam together. Wrap dough mixture with Saran® wrap and chill for an hour.

Remove the dough from the icebox. Take pieces off and roll into small balls. Take a tiny thimble or spoon and make a little intent, then fill the indent with apricot jam (or your favorite jam).

Put cookie rounds on a large cookie sheet and bake at 350°F for 10 minutes, watching carefully. The edges should be a little tan when done. A very pretty cookie!

Norey's Note:

These were the first Christmas cookies that my mother would make every year. We used to take her sewing thimble, dip it in flour, and make a little hole which we would fill with apricot jam. So delicious!

Chocolate Macaroons

1 14-ounce can condensed milk

1 teaspoon Karo syrup

16 ounces chocolate chips

2 cups coconut

1 cup chopped nuts (any kind)

½ cup golden raisins (chopped)

½ cup apricots (chopped)

½ cup dried cranberries (chopped)

1 tablespoon pure vanilla

½ teaspoon Kosher salt

TO PREPARE:

Pre-heat oven to 375°F. Spray baking sheet with oil as <u>these cookies burn easily</u>. Melt half of the chocolate chips, then mix all ingredients together and drop spoonfuls (slightly larger than a quarter) onto baking sheet.

Cook 8–9 minutes, watching cookies carefully. These cookies will last for weeks in a ziplock freezer bag.

Fantastic Chocolate Chip, Raisin & Oatmeal Cookies

2 sticks butter
1 cup light brown sugar
½ cup sugar
2 eggs
1 teaspoon instant coffee
1 teaspoon salt
1 teaspoon cinnamon
1 teaspoon baking soda
1 cup oatmeal
1 ½ cups flour
1 cup Rice Krispies®
1 cup chocolate chips
1 cup golden raisins
½ cup pecans (chopped)

TO PREPARE:

Combine butter with brown sugar and white sugar in a mix master, then add eggs one at a time. Sift together salt, cinnamon, baking soda, and flour into the mixture. Add raisins, oatmeal, Rice Krispies®, and chocolate chips. (I also like to add ½ cup pecans and 1 teaspoon instant coffee!)

Put spoonfuls of dough on a cookie sheet, leaving room between for spreading. Bake at 375°F for 8 minutes or until edges are slightly brown. Cool on a wire rack, and store in a cookie tin. They should last for several days, if there are any left after a few hours!

Norey's Note:

For those who love chocolate, raisins, and oatmeal, here is your dream cookie!

These cookies are thin and crispy. Be sure to space them far apart on the cookie sheet as they spread.

Lemon Cookies

2 sticks butter

1 cup sugar

3 ounces cream cheese

1 tablespoon lemon zest

2 tablespoons fresh lemon juice

1 egg

3 cups flour

1 teaspoon baking powder

TO PREPARE:

In a mix master, blend the butter, cream cheese, and sugar together. Add the egg, lemon zest, baking powder, lemon juice, and flour.

Put into a pastry bag and pipe dough in small rounds onto an ungreased cookie sheet, or simply roll a small amount in your hand and place on the cookie sheet. Dip the bottom of a small glass in flour so it won't stick, and use the bottom to flatten out the cookies. Bake at 375°F for 7–8 minutes, checking occasionally to ensure they don't burn. Remove from baking sheet and store in an airtight cookie tin.

Norey's Note:

I really like these pretty, delicate cookies. They are great as part of a "homemade" cookie platter.

They are also a nice gift wrapped in cellophane and tied with a pretty ribbon!

COOKIES

Oatmeal Shortbread with Sea Salt & Almonds

2 sticks butter (softened)

1 cup brown sugar

½ cup almonds

1 teaspoon pure vanilla

1 ½ cup flour

1 ½ cup oatmeal

½ teaspoon salt

1 tablespoon sea salt

TO PREPARE:

Pre-heat oven to 325°F. Cream together butter, brown sugar, salt, and vanilla. Add flour and oatmeal and mix well. Add a small amount of butter to a frying pan and sauté the almonds until golden brown, sprinkle with half of the sea salt then set aside.

Spread dough in a 9" x 13" glass baking pan. Add toasted almonds and sprinkle remaining sea salt on top. Bake for 15 minutes or until edges begin to brown slightly. Cut into squares to serve.

Sweet 'n Salty Butter Shortbread Cookies

2 sticks butter (salted or unsalted; room temperature)

⅔ cup powdered sugar

2 ½ cups all-purpose flour (sifted)

1 teaspoon salt

1 teaspoon vanilla

½ cup granulated sugar for sprinkling

½ cup course kosher salt for sprinkling

Norey's Note:

You can also add golden raisins to this recipe if you'd like!

TO PREPARE:

Mix ingredients together in a food processor. Refrigerate dough for 1 hour. Preheat oven to 350°F. Roll the dough out with a rolling pin, then cut into desired shapes using a cookie cutter. Sprinkle the cookies with a little granulated sugar and a touch of course salt.

Bake for 14 minutes or until just golden on the edges. <u>Watch carefully!</u> Let cool, and serve. These cookies store well in a tin!

Sweet Cream Cheese Puffs

Pastry:
2 cups unsifted flour
¼ teaspoon salt
1 cup unsalted butter (chilled, cubed)
½ cup sour cream
1 egg yolk

Sweet Cheese Filling:
8 ounces cream cheese (room temp)
1 egg
½ cup sugar
1 teaspoon vanilla
1 teaspoon finely grated lemon zest

TO PREPARE:

Mix flour and salt in a bowl, then combine with chilled butter pieces using a food processor, processing until the mixture has the appearance of small dried peas. In a separate bowl, combine the sour cream and egg yolk, then add into the flour mixture and continue to process until it forms a large ball of dough. Divide the ball into two pieces, flatten into discs, and chill at least 4 hours (overnight is best!).

Meanwhile, blend all filling ingredients together. Once dough has chilled, place each disc on a floured surface and roll until slightly thinner than ⅛ inch. Cut into 3-inch squares and place 1 heaping teaspoon of filling in the center of each square. Press opposite corners together to create puffs.

Chill puffs in refrigerator for 30 minutes, then bake at 375°F for 25–30 minutes. Sprinkle with powdered sugar.

Norey's Note:

These little sweet cheese puffs freeze very well if you need to make them ahead of time!

Walnut Butter Melts

2 sticks butter

1 cup sugar

2 cups walnuts

2 cups flour

1 tablespoon pure vanilla

1 teaspoon salt

2 cups confectioner's sugar

Norey's Note:

My Mother made these delicious cookies all the time, especially at Christmas to go along with the medley of sweets in cookie baskets for her friends.

These make a terrific gift!

TO PREPARE:

Chop the walnuts semi-finely in a food processor. Setting the confectioner's sugar aside, combine all other ingredients together with walnuts in a bowl. Form into balls with your hands. I like to form small ones so it's a one-bite cookie, but you can make them any size you want.

Place balls on a cookie sheet and bake at 325°F for about 30 minutes. As with all cookies, watch them carefully. The bottom of the cookie should be a tan color when done. Let them cool for 15 minutes and then roll each cookie in confectioner's sugar.

Other Desserts

I have often wondered if it would be interesting to have a dinner party with only desserts!! Or worse yet, serve dessert as a first course... I know it is a crazy idea but if you have some friends who are dessert freaks, just imagine their delight if the dinner was a variety of their favorite sweets! Of course, they can get it down with a glass of champagne.

I am a sweetaholic!! Hence, there are many "sweets" in this cookbook. A dessert is important as it is the last impression you make on your guests. Everyone is relaxed after a good meal and a sweet of some kind puts the "cap" on your evening.

Depending on the season and type of meal you choose, this will help to determine the dessert you create. In summer it is nice to have fresh fruit or a pudding with berries. When I make my Peach Bread Pudding (pg. 154), it is always a huge hit. In colder months, you might consider warm Sticky Toffee Pudding Cake (pg. 162) or warm Chocolate Bread Pudding (pg. 151) with fresh whipped cream on top.

If a recipe calls for whipped cream, <u>always</u> make it fresh. There is a huge difference from canned whipped cream! Powdered sugar sprinkled on top of the dessert and plate adds a nice touch. Also, I love to put fresh mint on my summer desserts.

A good espresso, tea, or after dinner liquor is the final touch with a small piece of dark chocolate. Good night everyone!!

OTHER DESSERTS

Apple Cream Cheese Torte

SERVES: 8

2 or 3 honeycrisp apples (peeled & sliced)

2 large eggs

1 tablespoon water (cold)

2 8-ounce packages cream cheese (softened)

½ cup sugar

⅓ cup brown sugar

1 teaspoon cinnamon

½ teaspoon kosher salt

2 teaspoons pure vanilla

Crust:

1 stick butter (cold)

1 teaspoon pure vanilla

1 ½ cups flour

½ cup sugar

Norey's Note:

I just love this dessert, it's great during apple season!

TO PREPARE:

Crust: Put crust ingredients into a food processor and pulse until a ball forms. Press into a 9-inch springform pan to form a crust and bake at 350°F for 5–6 minutes. Let cool.

While the crust bakes, put sugar, cream cheese, and eggs into a food processor or mixer and beat until smooth. Add 1 teaspoon vanilla. Pour into crust and bake at 400°F for 10 minutes.

Remove torte from oven. In a small bowl, mix sliced apples, brown sugar, cinnamon, and 1 teaspoon vanilla. Spread on top of the cream cheese mixture. Reduce heat to 350°F and bake for 40 minutes or until a knife inserted in the center comes out clean. Let cool, then cover and refrigerate until ready to serve.

Baked Caramelized Pears

SERVES: 6

- 3 tablespoons butter (melted)
- 6 large Bosc pears (somewhat ripe; stems on)
- ½ cup heavy cream
- 1 cup sugar
- 1 teaspoon kosher salt

TO PREPARE:

Pre-heat oven to 375°F. Peel the pears, making sure to keep stems on. Cut in half and remove any seeds. Line a pan with aluminum foil coated with half of the melted butter, and arrange pears on pan cut-side down. Brush remaining melted butter on top of the pears and sprinkle with sugar. Bake for 30 minutes or until pears are somewhat soft and a rich caramel color.

Place two baked pear halves on each plate, facing in opposite directions. Drizzle hot Bourbon Sauce (pg. 140) on top. Finish with a dollop of fresh whipped cream, or drizzle a bit of heavy cream on the plate before you place the pears.

A shortbread cookie on the side works perfectly! Try serving each pear with one of my Sweet 'n Salty Butter Shortbread Cookies on pg. 184)

Norey's Note:

This is truly a gorgeous dessert, especially during the holidays.

I make this recipe all the time. It's very satisfying!

You can use store bought caramel sauce drizzled over them too, if you like!

DESSERTS

Cream Cheese Key Lime Pie

SERVES: 10

1 cup key lime juice

zest of 2 limes

2 eggs

3 egg yolks

1 8-ounce package cream cheese (softened to room temp)

2 cans condensed milk

Crust:

1 stick butter

2 cups honey graham cracker crumbs

½ cup sugar

½ teaspoon cinnamon

TO PREPARE:

Crust: Pre-heat oven to 350°F. Melt butter in microwave and mix with graham cracker crumbs, sugar, and cinnamon. Press crust into a 10-inch springform pan.

Mix remaining ingredients together in a mix master, making sure that the cream cheese has blended well. Pour mixture into prepared crust.

Bake for 20 minutes. Serve with a sprig of fresh mint or fresh blueberries for a garnish.

Norey's Note:

The cream cheese really gives the recipe a lift!

DESSERTS

Plum & Blueberry Tart

SERVES: 8

Crust:

1 stick butter

1 tablespoon sugar

1 tablespoon apple cider vinegar

1 cup flour

Filling:

2 cups blueberries

1 cup plums (peeled, sliced)

1 cup sugar

½ teaspoon cinnamon

TO PREPARE:

Crust: Mix ingredients in a mix master to create a dough. Set aside ¼ of the mixuture to use separately. Press the rest of the dough into a 9-inch springform pan.

Toss the filling ingredients together until the blueberries and plum slices are thoroughly coated, then pour into the springform pan. Take the remaining dough and crumble it on top of the mixture.

Bake at 400°F for about 50 minutes or until crumbled crust is golden-brown. Serve with vanilla ice cream!

Norey's Note:

This is a delicious tart which originated from my friend Laurie Grauer. I put my own spin on it.

It is the perfect summer dessert when the fruits are in season!

Velvet Cream Pudding

SERVES: 8

1 ½ packets unflavored gelatin

¼ cup water

8 ounces cream cheese (room temperature)

1 cup sour cream

2 cups heavy cream

2 cups sugar

2 teaspoons pure vanilla

TO PREPARE:

Stir gelatin in ¼ cup water until dissolved. Set aside.

Heat heavy cream and sugar in a medium saucepan over medium heat. When mixture is hot, stir in dissolved gelatin. Put saucepan in refrigerator for 30 minutes to cool.

Mix cream cheese with sour cream in a mix master and add vanilla. Add the heavy cream and sugar mixture and stir until well blended. Cover with Saran® wrap and return to refrigerator for 3–4 hours (overnight is best!) until thick.

Serve in a small bowl with fresh berries. This pudding will last 4–5 days stored in the icebox.

Norey's Note:

This dessert was a big hit at the restaurant. Put pudding into pretty glass bowls for a nice effect.

Delicious served with my Shortbread Cookies on pg. 184!

White Chocolate Coeur à la Crème

SERVES: 6

1 cup heavy cream

1 cup powdered sugar

1 8-ounce package of cream cheese (softened)

5 ounces white chocolate (melted)

1 tablespoon pure vanilla

1 pint fresh raspberries

TO PREPARE:

In a stand mixer, beat cream cheese, heavy cream, and powdered sugar together until thick. Add the melted white chocolate and vanilla. Put mixture into small individual glass bowls and refrigerate for several hours. Top with fresh raspberries and a sprig of fresh mint.

Norey's Note:

A bit different, and especially great if you like white chocolate!

Appendix

Here are some of the appliances I use most often. They are my best friends in my kitchen!

BLENDER

FOOD PROCESSOR

EMULSIFIER	STAND MIXER OR A MIX MASTER

Recipe Index

Hors d'Oeuvres

- A Word About Hors d'Oeuvres 15
- Basil & Tomato Rounds 16
- Cream Cheese Cinnamon Sticks 19
- Cream Cheese Dip with Almonds & Endive 20
- Deviled Eggs 22
- Fresh Dates with Cream Cheese & Almonds 23
- Hummus (My Way!) 24
- Hungarian Cheese Spread 26
- Kielbasa Bites with White Wine 27
- Mini BLTs with Avocado 29
- Mini Ham Salad Bites 30
- Mini Roasted Potatoes 31
- Nana's German Meatballs 32
- Nina's Onion Cornbread 33
- Pear & Goat Cheese Bruschetta 34
- Roasted Plum Tomato Bruschetta 37
- Special Chicken Salad 38

Soups

- A Word About Soups 41
- African Sweet Potato Soup 42
- Black Bean Soup with Beer & Spices 43
- Brandied Chestnut Soup with Apples 44
- Cold Carrot Soup with Honey & Ginger 47
- Clam Chowder 48
- Corn Chowder (My Way!) 51
- Cream of Tomato Soup 52
- Fresh French Lentil Soup (My Way!) 54
- Fresh Mint, Avocado & Baby Pea Soup 55
- Greek Vegetable Soup 57
- Jellied White Gazpacho 58
- Mushroom Bisque with Port 59
- Roasted Butternut Squash & Apple Soup 60
- Roasted Cauliflower & Apple Soup 63
- Roasted Red Pepper & Tomato Soup 64

Salads

A Word About Salads	67
Arugula & Pomegranate Salad	68
Bib & Boston Salad with Bleu Cheese & Almonds	69
Chopped Baby Kale Salad with Avocado	71
Chopped Kitchen Sink Salad	72
Chopped Wedge Salad with Arugula & Bleu Cheese	74
Elegant Caesar Salad	75
End of Summer Salad	77
Grandma Benner's Salad with Hot Dressing	78
Hot Vegetable Salad with Arugula	81
My Version of Waldorf Salad	82
Quinoa Salad with Fresh Veggies & Feta	85
Roasted Butternut Squash & Arugula Salad	86

Sandwiches

A Word About Sandwiches	89
The Art of Making a Perfect Tea Sandwich	90
Cinnamon Raisin Bread with Cream Cheese & Chutney	92
Day After Thanksgiving Sandwich	94
Egg Salad Sandwich with Bacon, Arugula & Tomato	95
Goat Cheese & Tomato Sandwiches	96
Grilled Peanut Butter & Jelly	97
Smoked Salmon Sandwich	98

Entrées

A Word About Entrées	101
Chicken Florentine	102
Chicken Marsala with Mushrooms, Capers & Leeks	103
Chicken Paillard with Grilled Lemon Artichokes	104
Chicken Pot Pie My Way	107
Chinese Orange Shrimp	108
Judy Cullen's Maryland Crab Cakes	109
Lemon Chicken with Arugula & Capers	110
Norey's Famous Spaghetti and Meat Sauce	113
Norey's Meatloaf	114

Oriental Lamb Chops	115
Poor Man's Potato Pie	116
Pork Paillard with Hot Pepper Jelly	118
Pork Tenderloin with an Asian Twist	119
Rosemary Beef Stew the Italian Way	120
Stuffed Shells My Way	121
Tyler's Asian Chicken Lettuce Wraps	122

Vegetables

A Word About Vegetables	125
French String Beans with Asian Sauce	126
German Golden & Red Beets	127
Grilled Baby Artichkes with Lemon	128
Honey Ginger Carrot Purée	129
Rice Casserole	130
Tomato Pudding	131
Sautéed Brussels Sprouts & Leeks with Toasted Almonds	133

Dressings & Sauces

A Word About Dressings & Sauces	135
1000 Island Dressing	136
Caesar Salad Dressing	136
David's Sesame Ginger Dressing	137
Honey Lemon Vinaigrette	137
Nina's Roquefort & Anchovy Dressing	138
Spinach Salad Dressing from the Black Pearl	138
Sweet Balsamic Dressing	139
Asian Sweet Sauce	139
A Different Pesto	140
Bourbon Sauce	140
Lime Sauce	141
Norey's Beurre Blanc Sauce	141
Peanut Sauce (My Way!)	142
Homemade Bread Crumbs	142
Roasted Pecans	143
Salted Toasted Almonds	143

Bread Pudding

A Word About Bread Pudding 145
Artichoke & Baby Broccoli with Goat & Manchego Cheese 146
Mushroom, Onion & Cheese Bread Pudding 147
Roasted Corn, Onion & Cheddar Bread Pudding 148
Chocolate Raisin Bread Pudding 151
Coconut Bread Pudding 152
Fresh Blueberry Brea5 Pudding 153
Fresh Peach Bread Pudding 154
Peanut Butter & Jelly Bread Pudding 155
Pineapple Almond Bread Pudding 156
Vanilla Bourbon Bread Pudding 157

Cakes

A Word About Cakes 159
Best Lemon Cream Cheese Pound Cake 160
Chocolate Raisin Sticky Toffee Pudding Cake 162
Dense Dark Chocolate Mini Cupcakes 163
Ginger Cheesecake 164
Mom's Honeycrisp Apple Cake with Walnuts 167
Peanut Butter Cream Cheese Cake 168
Sour Cream Butter Cake 171
Ultimate Carrot Cake 172

Cookies

A Word About Cookies 175
Almond Apricot Shortbread 176
Butter Roll Cookies with Apricot Jam 178
Chocolate Macaroons 179
Fantastic Chocolate Chip, Raisin & Oatmeal Cookies 180
Lemon Cookies 181
Oatmeal Shortbread with Sea Salt & Almonds 183
Sweet 'n Salty Butter Shortbread Cookies 184
Sweet Cream Cheese Puffs 186
Walnut Butter Melts 187

Other Desserts

    A Word About Other Desserts...189

    Apple Cream Cheese Torte 190

    Baked Caramelized Pears 191

    Cream Cheese Key Lime Pie 192

    Plum & Blueberry Tart 195

    Velvet Cream Pudding 196

    White Chocolate Coeur à la Crème...197

Appendix

    Appliances Used 198

Notes

Notes

Notes